The *Ancestral Lines* of
JAMES EDWARD AIGUIER

Dr. James E. Aiguier in the 1930s. Note that the gold key on his watch chain is that of the Sigma Xi National Honorary Scientific Society, awarded to him on March 14, 1917, in his senior year at the Evans Institute of the University of Pennsylvania.

The *Ancestral Lines* of
JAMES EDWARD AIGUIER

Harry W. Havemeyer

PRIVATELY PRINTED, NEW YORK

For all of Favie's descendants.

CONTENTS

Four immigrants came to the New World under entirely different circumstances and in different centuries. None of the four could have been called a leader; each came as a follower with a group of others. One never intended to remain, but because of an injury received in battle he never returned to the land of his birth.

The first to arrive in the Western Hemisphere were Joshua Carter and Zechariah Field, English Puritans who joined the Great Puritan Migration of the 1630s, sailing to Boston, Massachusetts, as two of 20,000 immigrants who would make the two-month voyage in that decade.

A century and a half later, in 1781, Jean François Arnoux, a surgeon on the French navy frigate *La Diligente*, sailed with the fleet of Admiral de Grasse to help General George Washington defeat Great Britain in the War of Independence. Injured in the battle of Yorktown, Arnoux remained in the United States and in Canada for the rest of his life.

Shortly thereafter, in the early nineteenth century, another Frenchman, Jean Baptiste Aiguier, came to New York City with a group of immigrants from the port of Marseilles—we don't know why. He was a confectioner by trade and may have wanted more opportunities than a life in a Provençal village in the Pays des Aiguiers, where he was born, would permit.

Arnoux and Aiguier, who never knew each other, only spoke French when they emigrated. Carter and Field, of course, spoke English, as did their many descendants. However, one of these, Carter's great grandson John Carter, at the age of nine was kidnapped by the French-led expedition to raid the community at Deerfield, Massachusetts, in 1704. Taken as a prisoner to Montreal in French Canada, he was educated by an order of monks and in adulthood became Jean Chartier, a citizen of New France and a Roman Catholic with an excellent command of his new language.

What follows is the story of these four immigrants and their offspring. As they each lived at the heart of the American story from 1630 to 1977, important moments of American history in which they participated are recalled, such as the Deerfield Massacre, the battle at Yorktown, and the draft riots in New York City in the 1860s, to name a few.

The family lines of all four end in this account with James Edward Aiguier, my father-in-law, who died in 1977. Favie (as I called him) was a direct descendant of all four. He was very interested in his forbearers, particularly those of his mother, the Demarest family, which has been thoroughly researched. This account is of his paternal ancestors, the Aiguier, Arnoux, Carter/Chartier, and Field lines, of which he knew much less. In fact, I do not believe he knew anything of his Carter/Chartier and Field ancestry.

That discovery, in fact, was made very recently by his granddaughter, my daughter Ann Havemeyer, to whom I owe great thanks for all the research she has done to confirm this connection. I would also like to thank my daughter, Catherine Havemeyer, for discovering two other immigrant ancestors, as well as for designing and producing the book, and my granddaughter Lizzie Strumolo for the many hours she spent putting my manuscript on her computer. All three, of course, are descendants of the four immigrants. Finally, my thanks go to Peter Rooney who provided the important index.

Harry W. Havemeyer
July 2012

PART I

Colonies of New England
and New France

1630–1763

The Great Puritan Migration

At the sound of a cannon in the early morning of a windy March day in the year 1630, the English ship *Arbella* weighed anchor in the Solent and slowly moved westward to begin a journey to the new colony of Massachusetts Bay. She carried twenty-eight guns and was the flagship for sixteen other ships that would cross the Atlantic Ocean that year for the new colony. On board *Arbella* were aristocrats from the County of Rutland with the names Johnson, Fiennes, Bradstreet, Dudley, and Saltanstall; and a Suffolk County lawyer named John Winthrop, who would become the governor of the new colony. Most of the travelers were of lesser rank, but only a few were poor people. Most came from East Anglia, the eastern part of southern England, and they had no intentions of ever returning to the homeland. Thus began the Great Puritan Migration, which for size, wealth, and organization was without precedent in England's colonization of North America.

These seventeen ships were the vanguard of nearly two hundred ships, each carrying about one hundred English Puritans, which brought 21,000 people to Massachusetts from 1630 to 1641.* This mass migration ended as abruptly as it began due to the beginning of the English Civil War when some Puritans returned to England to fight in the Parliamentary army against King Charles. It did resume again, at a much slower pace, after the restoration of Charles II in 1660. By 1700, the English population in New England had reached one hundred thousand.

They were an amazingly homogenous group of men, women, and children who multiplied at a very high rate with families averaging seven to eight children. Healthy women married young and bore offspring quickly. Death rates of the young were high, but the need for labor was without end. The families expanded throughout southern New England searching for arable land. In this hilly country, flat land near a major river was at a great premium; such sites became new villages and later towns. In this rapid expansion the colonists were looking for economic improvement and personal security.

Historian David Hackett Fischer describes the English Puritans as coming "from the middle ranks of their society, and traveling in family groups. The heads of these families tended to be exceptionally literate, highly skilled, and heavily urban in their English origins. They were people of substance, charac-

---

* Only one vessel was lost in ten years.

ter, and deep personal piety."[1] They were yeomen, husbandmen, artisans, crafts-men, merchants, and traders. Three-quarters of the adult males were said to pay the way for their families.

Why did this exodus of biblical proportions take place in this decade? The answer lies in the Puritan's belief in the concept of "ordered liberty" and how their lives in England were being changed against their will by a monarch whose views and beliefs were radically different. Whig historians called this period the "eleven years of tyranny." "Ordered liberty" for these Puritans em-bodied four concepts: collective liberty, individual liberty, soul liberty relating to religious belief, and freedom from tyranny by the governing authority. In a large part of England, but centered in East Anglia, they were losing all four due to the policies and actions of their king and his ministers.[2]

In 1625 Charles I inherited the throne of England, succeeding his father James I who was strongly Protestant, as was his predecessor Elizabeth I. Al-though Charles was nominally a Protestant, he married Henrietta Maria, daughter of Henry IV of France, a Roman Catholic princess who came to England with a Roman Catholic entourage. She was bitterly disliked by most English, who thought that Charles was or was becoming a "closet Catholic" as they watched him favor "popish" practices for the Church of England and ap-point "popish" bishops such as William Laud in 1633 to become Archbishop of Canterbury. Laud began to purge the church of its Puritan-leaning minis-ters and insist on church ritual that offended them and that the Puritan-dom-inated Parliament had prohibited, such as the observance of Christmas, Easter, saints' and holy days. For Puritans, who believed that God did not act through rituals, traditions, or church hierarchies, but instead acted directly on each in-dividual by an offer of saving grace, it was God's Word as read in the Bible and preached by the minister that counted. Ninety Puritan ministers would carry that message to New England during the Great Migration. The king and arch-bishop were irrelevant to their lives unless they were interfering with them—which they were beginning to do.

If this interference was not enough, King Charles I from the beginning of his reign struggled with a Puritan Parliament that increasingly disagreed with him. In 1629 he dissolved the Parliament altogether and for eleven years ruled alone as a tyrant. Those eleven years coincided with the Great Migration to Massachusetts. John Winthrop, about to sail away from his beloved Suffolk village forever, said: "The land has grown weary of her Inhabitants, so as man which is most precious of all the Creatures, is here more vile and base than the earth they tread upon." It was time to leave. Their belief in "ordered liberty" had been violated by the king and state.[3]

Joshua Carter and Zechariah Field
Puritan Immigrants 1630–1675

Among the sixteen other vessels that joined *Arbella* and John Winthrop on the journey to Massachusetts Bay in March 1630 was *Mary and John*, sailing from Weymouth with a stop at Plymouth to pick up more immigrants. The Reverend John White had organized a group of Puritans from his church in Dorchester in Dorset County. One, Roger Ludlow, was the owner of the ship. Two others, the Reverends John Warham and John Maverick, neighborhood rectors, would lead an expedition of 140 people to Massachusetts Bay sailing down the English Channel on the tide to meet up with the main group coming from Southampton. One of the 140 people aboard called the Dorchester group was Joshua Carter. He could have come from the town itself or from the neighboring villages. He was single, young and wanting a new life. The times had become hard in parts of England as the wool trade was in decline causing a depression and scarcity of work. For Reverends White, Warham, and Maverick, however, the reason for the voyage to colonize America was religion: "the most eminent and desirable end of planting colonies is the propagation of religion."[4] The new Bishop of Bath and Wells in 1626 was none other than William Laud on his way to being Archbishop of Canterbury, who was constantly complaining about Puritans who disregarded the rules of the Church of England, a forerunner of his actions to come.

The voyage of *Mary and John* in 1630 was never recounted as was that of *Arbella* by Governor Winthrop, but similarities existed. The former was a larger ship of 400 tons, able to carry the 140 emigrants in addition to the crew under Thomas Squibb, the master. She was faster with sufficient cannons to keep away pirates, which were regularly on the prowl in the seventeenth century for any unarmed vessel. It was expected that the voyage to Massachusetts Bay would take over ten weeks and sufficient provisions for that time required a substantial cargo. The planned course out of Plymouth was to the Isles of Scilly and then on the northern route, north of 46° latitude across the Atlantic Ocean to the Grand Banks of Newfoundland. This route–the great circle route–was

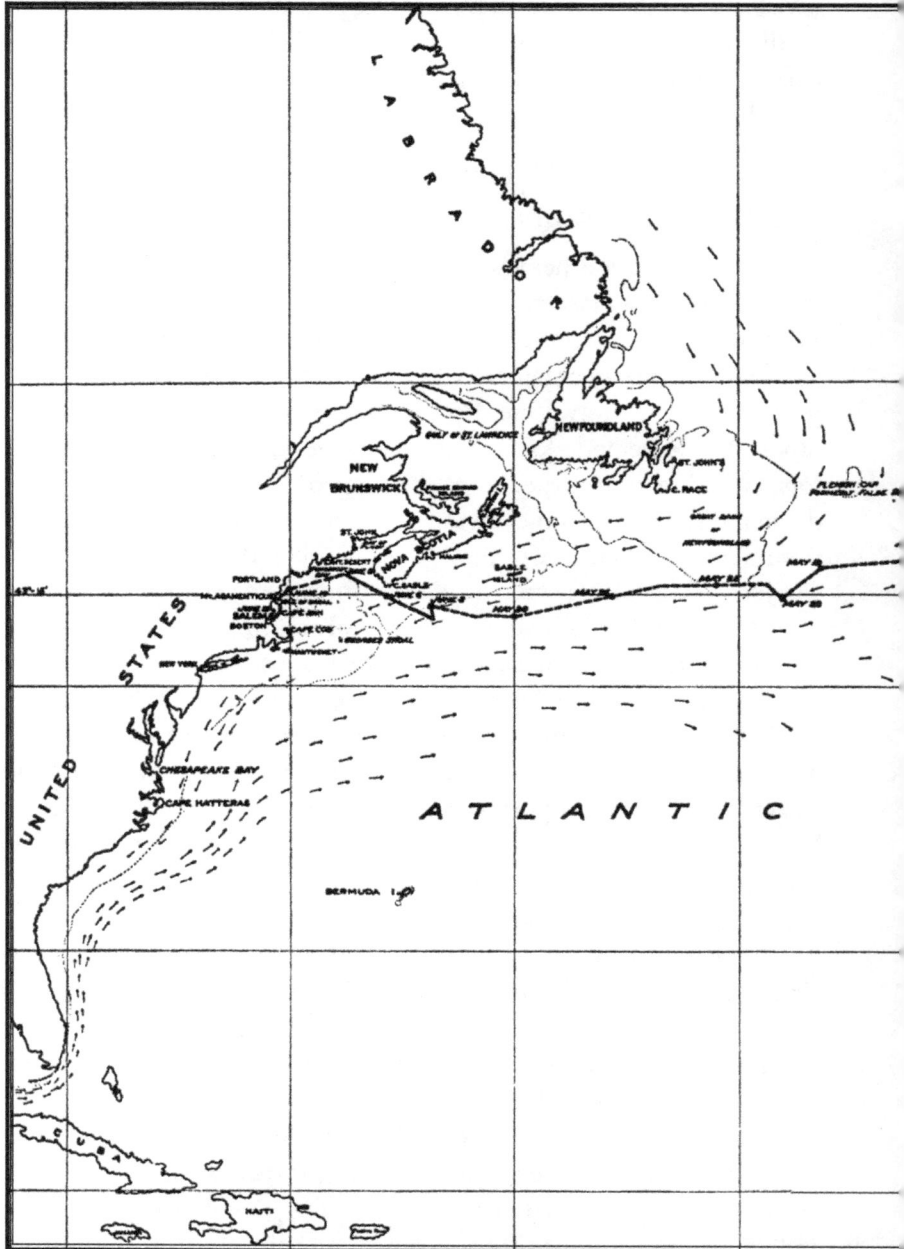

Course taken by *Mary and John,* 29 March 1630 to 30 May 1630- 60 days

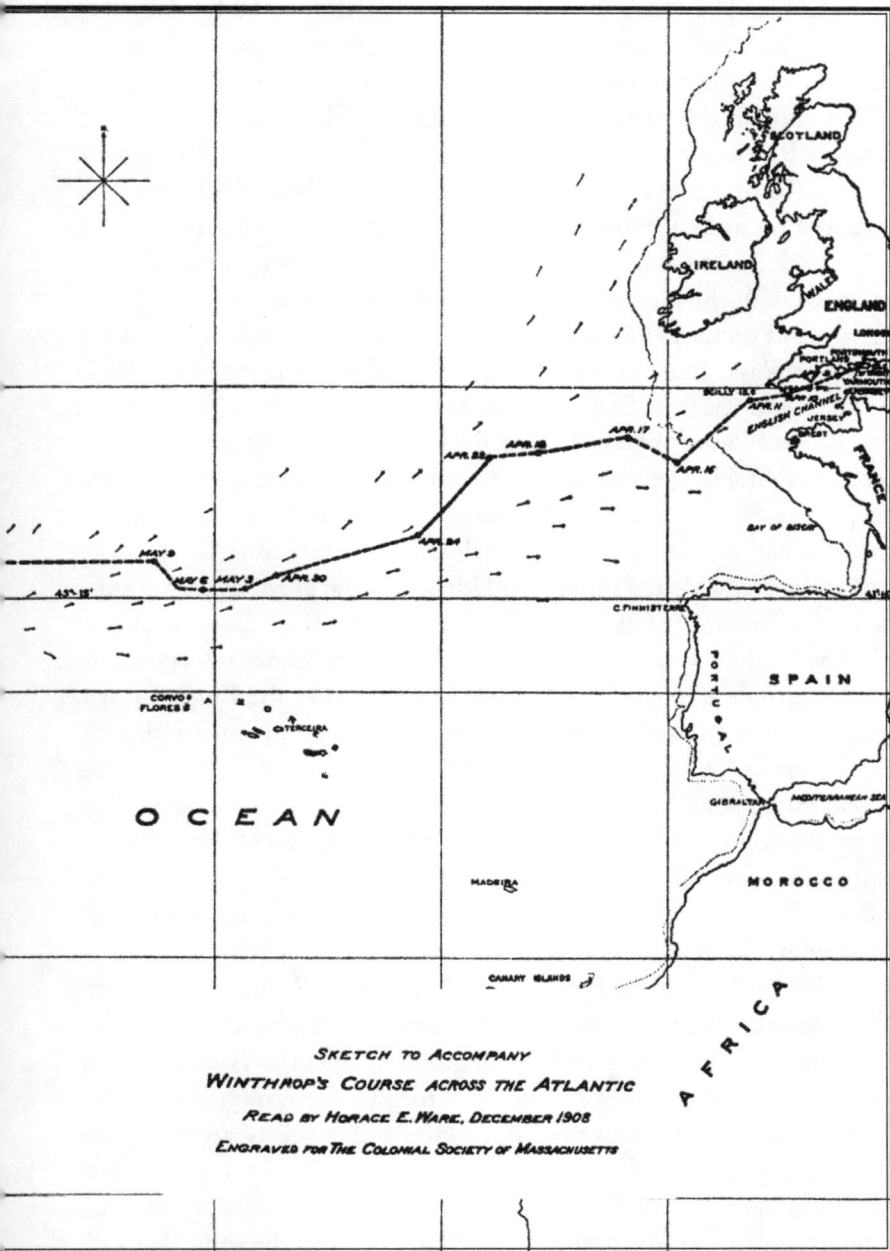

SKETCH TO ACCOMPANY
WINTHROP'S COURSE ACROSS THE ATLANTIC
READ BY HORACE E. WARE, DECEMBER 1908
ENGRAVED FOR THE COLONIAL SOCIETY OF MASSACHUSETTS

the shortest, but could be stormy. It avoided the worst of the Gulf Stream eastbound current which for a square-rigged vessel, which could not sail close to the direction of the wind, was essential. Should the wind be southwest, a westbound sailing craft in the eastbound Gulf Stream might actually be pushed back to Europe. Risking storms was better than this. Once in the Grand Banks there was often fog to contend with, then Sable Island off Nova Scotia to avoid going aground–hundreds of shipwrecks occurred there–and finally, the Gulf of Maine and Massachusetts Bay. That twenty thousand Puritans chose this voyage in the 1630s with the loss of only one ship was extraordinary.

Where to land presented another problem. Captain Squibb's ship was the first to arrive in the Bay that season–ships did not make winter crossings then–and on Sunday, May 30th, *Mary and John* had no pilot and no instructions. Boston was and is a harbor filled with small islands and the captain's boat was of very deep draught. His decision was to drop anchor off Nantasket Point and unload his passengers on to barren Mattapan Neck, a very bleak and inhospitable shore. He had contracted to deliver them to a spot along the Charles River that the Reverend White's friend had identified the previous year as suitable for a new community, but had reneged on his contract. Because it was suitable for the cattle they had brought with them, they chose reluctantly to remain in Mattapan and renamed the area Dorchester after the English town. All summer they worked hard to prepare this treeless land for winter with little help from Governor Winthrop, who had arrived in Charleston three weeks after they did and claimed Boston peninsula to be the colony's capital. That they survived the coming winter was a miracle itself; only one of the 140 died. Their small community attracted only a few new residents. One of these settlers to join the Dorchester group and later make his mark was not from Dorset or Somerset at all; he came from the north of England in Yorkshire.

Born in 1596 in the town of East Ardsley in the West Riding of Yorkshire, Zechariah Field was the son of John and grandson of John Field, an astronomer. Little is known of his younger years but growing up in the West Yorkshire moors would have trained him for a life of hardship. These moors, made famous in the nineteenth century by the Brontë family of novelists, are one of the harshest, most barren parts of England, as different from Dorset and Somerset as night is to day. Zechariah left this land in 1630 at age 34, traveling through Wales to sail from Bristol to Boston. He could have been on the ship *Lion* with Captain Pierce, which Governor Winthrop commissioned to bring much

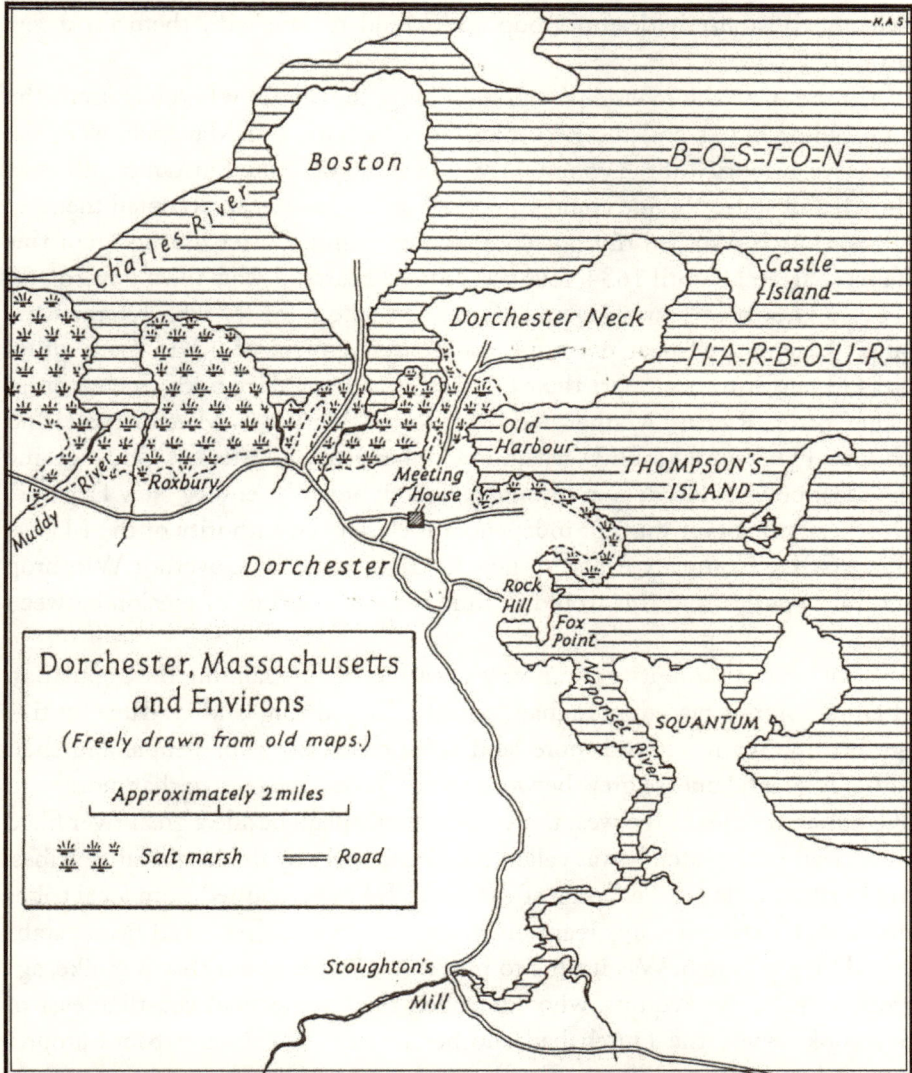

Dorchester, Massachusetts
and Environs
(Freely drawn from old maps.)

Approximately 2 miles

Salt marsh　　Road

The *Mary and John*'s passengers disembarked on Dorchester Neck in June 1630 and proceeded to settle on the mainland.

needed supplies form Bristol to Boston that winter of 1630–31. Its safe arrival was in time to save the Massachusetts Bay Colony from starvation during that severe winter. In any event Zechariah chose to join the Dorchester group rather than the Boston/Charleston group and would remain with them for a few years.

In the "new" Dorchester the first building to be built was the church. The two leading elders and the two ministers, Warham and Maverick, were the executive authority of the community in keeping with the Puritan tradition of church and state. No one could vote at all unless he was an accepted member of the church. Women did not vote. Young Joshua Carter did not gain this status as freeman until 1634, four years after his arrival. This town governance became known as New England Way. Thus the minister who retained the pulpit became the most powerful leader, and laymen, who had many other tasks to perform to support their families, took secondary roles. Such men as John Cotton, Richard Mather, and later Cotton Mather, in Massachusetts and Thomas Hooker and John Warham in Connecticut, ministers of God, became the most powerful leaders in seventeen and eighteenth century New England. Dorchester however was not independent. Under the authority of the Massachusetts Bay Company it had to take instructions from Governor Winthrop and his deputies, and this would in time become a source of tension between them.

The new community grew. Five years after the first landing the population of Dorchester increased more than fourfold. The existing land available for tillage became worn out and more land was needed both for people and their cattle. A general unease grew between towns. It became known that more than one hundred miles to the west there was a fertile plain beside a great river filled with clean fresh water. It was called the Great River by the local Native tribes; the Puritans called it the Connecticut River. They also learned from local tribes that about sixty miles upstream on this river a trading post had been established by the Dutch. Was it time to move? And what about that war-like, aggressive tribe, the Pequots, who controlled the Connecticut coastline east of Saybrook, where the Dutch had another fortress. The Native tribes around Boston had been friendly, but the Pequot would not be. They were constantly threatening the Saybrook fort as well as other Native tribes.

As the population grew around Boston, other groups began to look toward the Connecticut Valley as well. The most important of these was the group in

Newtown (Cambridge today) led the dynamic Reverend Thomas Hooker. It was Hooker's personality and standing that finally persuaded Governor Winthrop and the Court of Assistants to agree to groups in the Colony leaving the security provided by Massachusetts Bay. Hooker had been refused once, but he could be persuasive. Cotton Mather later wrote, "Hooker was able to do more with a word, or a look, than most other men could have done by a severer discipline."[5] In the summer of 1635 he was granted permission. Watertown and Dorchester soon thereafter were allowed to follow. Hooker also had become disenchanted with Massachusetts's theological practice of limiting the freemanship to church members. He would abolish this in Connecticut.

The first attempt of the Dorchester community to leave was almost a disaster. Their leaders were Roger Ludlow, the minister John Warham and Captain Mason. Ludlow was from a family of rank in Wiltshire and a member of the House of Commons. He had been a student of Balliol College, Oxford, and a member of the Inner Temple in London. With a party of twelve Dorchester men he had set off for the Connecticut River to scout for a suitable place for a community of about sixty men, women and children to settle. After about a hundred miles of mostly forest peopled by Native tribes, mostly Nipmucks, Mohegans and so-called river Indians, all of whom were friendly, the twelve white men finally reached the Great River near a place called Matianuck on the west bank about sixty miles north of the mouth. Here the Plymouth Colony had established a trading post and the group rested for ten days before leaving to find a settlement site. Ludlow decided that the best location for his new Dorchester was just north of the Plymouth post; the local Native tribe was on the east bank across the river. He claimed the land for the Massachusetts Bay Colony ignoring the Plymouth post and set about staking home lots and raising bivouacs.

Throughout the summer and early fall over sixty men, women and children mostly from Dorchester, but also from Newtown and Watertown, arrived at Matianuck. The word was getting around. A small vessel actually sailed around Cape Cod and up the Connecticut River to the site that summer. Unfortunately an early winter overtook the camp and by October 15 frost appeared, persuading Ludlow that, in order to survive, the group must return to Dorchester, Massachusetts for the winter. The twelve who came overland returned that way. One of these died drowning under the ice. The rest of the group took a boat downriver and around Cape Cod, a trip which took almost a month. Most

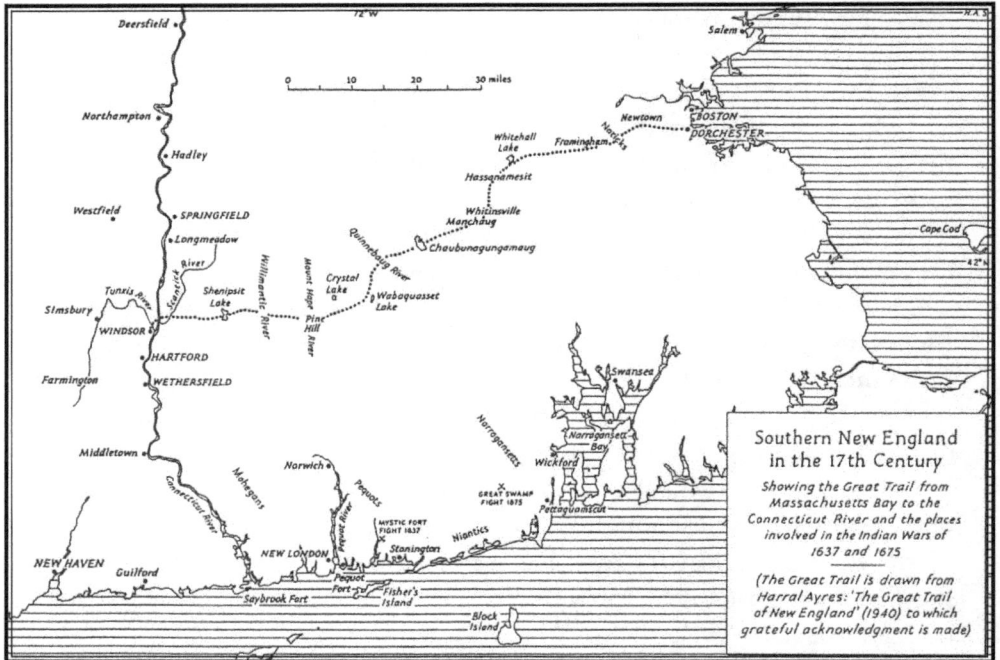

The route of exploration and settlement from Dorchester to Windsor in 1635 and 1636.

survived this ordeal but a few died of starvation, as did most of their cattle. Although we do not know the role of Joshua Carter, because he was single, young and strong, it is possible that he was one of Ludlow's twelve scouts who went overland to the river and returned with him.

After a depressing winter back in Dorchester, Ludlow started out west again in March 1636. Most people went overland by the forest trails that were now familiar to those who were repeating the journey. This second trip took place at the same time as a sister journey led by Thomas Hooker from New-town (Cambridge) to Saukiaug on the Great River. Zechariah Field was a part of this group. By the end of April both groups began to arrive; those with Ludlow to Matianuck, first renamed Dorchester and then Windsor, and those with Hooker to the Dutch fort ten miles down river, renamed Hartford. A few went further down to settle in Wethersfield. It was estimated that these three plantations in 1636, soon to be known as the Colony of Connecticut, consisted of 800 individuals in 160 to 170 families with up to 90 single men. The great majority of these came from Dorchester Massachusetts, and before that from Dorset, Somerset, and Devon in England.

During the past winter in conferences held in Boston, it was agreed between Ludlow and Hooker, on behalf of the settlers, and the Governor and the Court, on behalf of the Massachusetts Bay Colony, that the three Connecticut River settlements were too far away to be governed by Massachusetts and that a provisional government be established for one year, headed by Roger Ludlow. It was also agreed at that time that deputies would be elected to serve on the Commission who were freemen as in Massachusetts, but that they did not have to be members of the church. This was a significant difference insisted up by both Thomas Hooker and Roger Ludlow. It was the first break in the clerical hold on governance in New England and became in 1639 part of the new constitution of the Colony of Connecticut. The Dorchester group is given full credit for this historic act. Early the following year–1637–the name of their new home on the Great River was changed to Windsor to honor Roger Ludlow whose grandmother's family had that surname.

If Ludlow was the de facto governor of the new colony, Captain John Mason was its commander in chief. He saw to its defense by building a palisado–the Spanish word for fortified town–that partially exists today. It was sorely needed because in 1637 not all the Native tribes were friendly. The Pequot tribe (Algonquin for "destroyer") of coastal Connecticut had been on the warpath for several years and had slain several prominent English settlers. The tribe was disliked by most neighboring Natives including the Mohegans, so the settlers had allies in this war. In May Captain Mason sailed off down the Connecticut River to attack the Pequot fortress at Mystic on the Pequot River. His group consisted of seventy-seven men from the three villages of Windsor, Hartford and Wethersfield. In the group from Hartford was Zechariah Field who, being single and about forty, was a trusted lieutenant to Captain Mason and Captain John Underhill from Massachusetts, a well-known Indian fighter. Mason's group sailed down river to Saybrook where they were joined by the leader of that fort, Lion Gardiner, thence sailing east along the coast of Rhode Island to Narragansett Bay where the Native tribe hated the Pequots and would always fight them. From there an overland passage westbound would take them to Mystic, catching the Pequot by surprise, it was hoped, as the normal course would have been by water from Fishers Island Sound.

Captains Mason, Underhill, and Gardiner were all Low Country (Holland) veterans and seasoned professionals who had come to Massachusetts to provide some military expertise to the new settlement in the early 1630s. They were experts on how to destroy a fortress having had experience in the Thirty Years War against Spain. Gardiner would go on to acquire the island of that name in Long Island and settle in East Hampton near there. Underhill would fight the Natives that attacked early settlers in New Netherland, which the Dutch controlled. He was an Indian fighter for hire.

The task force approached the Mystic fort before dawn in the early hours of May 26, 1637. They had not been detected. The Natives were asleep and there were no guards in evidence. Mason took the eastern entrance and Underhill the western. Uncas, a former Pequot chief, who was now a Mohegan and deeply loyal to the English, had also come to guide the white men through the forest from Narragansett Bay. He had sixty of his Mohegan warriors and two hundred Narragansett warriors with him.

When Mason's group got to within ten yards of the eastern entrance, a dog barked, a Pequot spotted the attackers, and the fight was on. It was the intention of the English to burn the entire compound, which the Reverend Shepard called a "divine slaughter" and Mason labeled the "dreadful terror".[6] He set alight the thatch on top of the wigwams, and in no time the fort was blazing. It burned down within half an hour. Perhaps four hundred Pequot—men, women and children—were killed in the space of an hour. Only two English

The attack and massacre at Mystic Fort in May 1637 by Captain Mason and his men from Hartford, Connecticut, resulted in the death of four hundred Pequot men, women, and children. Their village was torched and destroyed in an hour.

soldiers were killed, with about twenty wounded. Ancestor Field must have witnessed this holocaust that substantially weakened the Pequot threat to the new settlements on the Great River.

The English task force returned to Fort Saybrook where they cared for the wounded, were welcomed by Captain Gardiner, and celebrated their victory. Then, it was a boat trip upriver to Hartford and Windsor, more celebrations and prayers of thanksgiving. Captain Mason made one more attack on that tribe shortly thereafter in a swamp near the mouth of the Quinnipiac River, where a new colony called New Haven had recently been established by the Reverend John Davenport and Theophilus Eaton. It would remain a separate colony from Connecticut until 1664. The Pequot chieftain was killed in Mason's attack and the tribe was completely dispersed.

With the end of the Pequot War in 1637 the English settlers and the other Native tribes in New England coexisted with only minor tension for another 38 years, at which time another tribe would go on the war path in King Philip's War of 1675. In Hartford at a special ceremony Thomas Hooker, minister of the church, presented Captain Mason with his military staff as the man of the hour. The following spring he was appointed Sergeant-Major General, commander in chief of all Connecticut forces, the outstanding military figure in Windsor and in Connecticut as a whole. The Windsor group went back to the hard work of settlement with few distractions.

While Captain Mason was fighting the last phase of the Pequot War, Roger Ludlow and William Phelps, for Windsor, and Mr. Prince, for the Plymouth Colony, were negotiating a solution to the land settlement in Matianuck on the West Bank of the Great River that first Plymouth and later the Dorchester group had claimed. The two began to bargain in February 1636 and agreed in May 1637, fourteen months later. During this time the Dorchester-Windsor planters were staking out claims through most of the area, and Plymouth was agreeing to take only a small meadow to the south for their settlers. The Windsor town surveyor, Matthew Grant, was in charge of surveying the homestead lots. The town clerk recorded them and reported them to the court in Hartford.

The home lots varied in size from 20 acres in the low end to nearly 800 acres at the top, depending on the grantees contribution to the community, his wealth, his social status and the size of his family. Thus it was that Joshua Carter, a single man, not wealthy, but of good standing, received a lot of 115

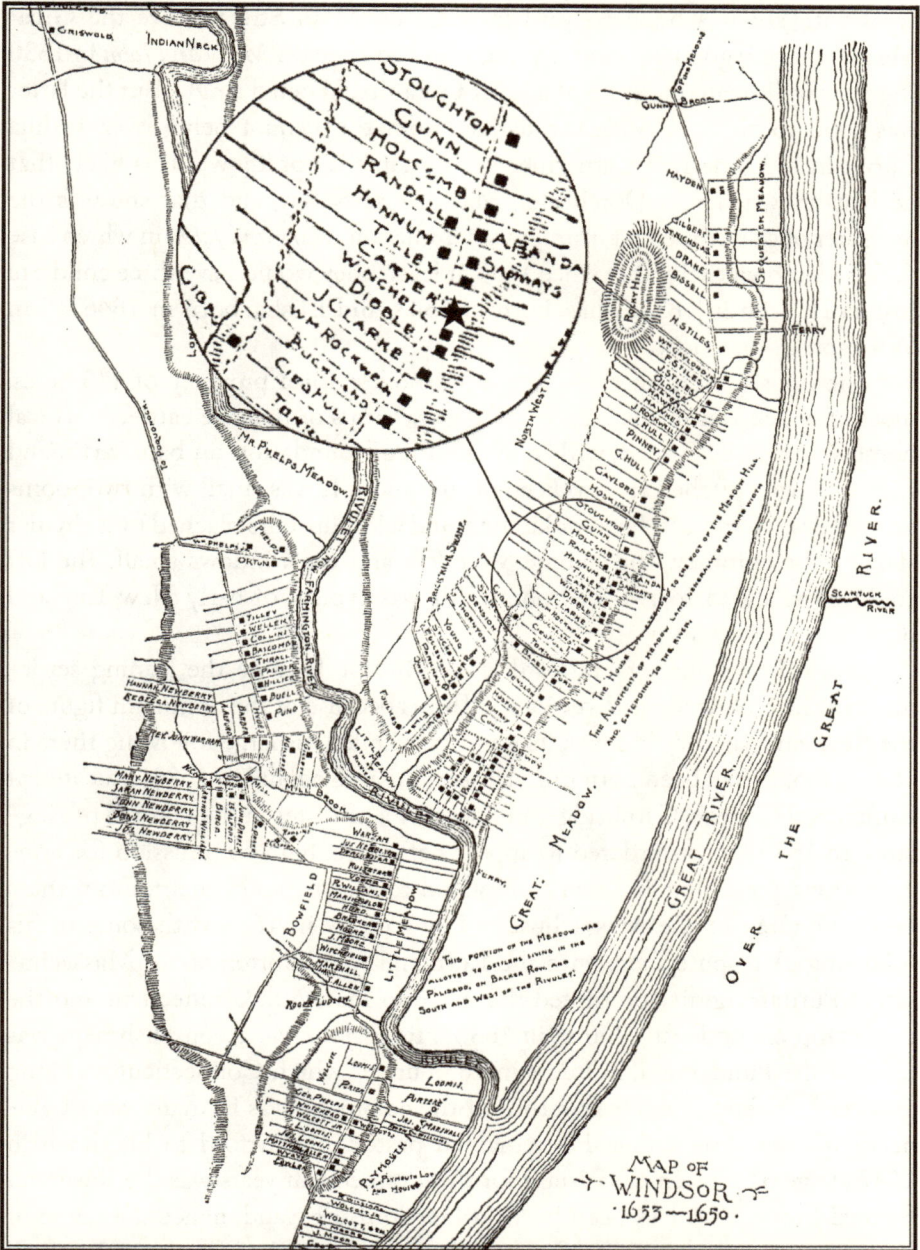

The map of Windsor, Connecticut, where the Carter family settled in 1636. His property is identified with a star.

acres with about a hundred yard frontage on Main Street above the Great Meadow, a very good location. Carter, who had been on *Mary and John* in 1630 was very well treated in spite of a lack of wealth and being single. But the latter was soon to change. With the danger from the Pequot being over, Joshua Carter in 1637 married Catherine- her surname is not known. It is likely that he had known her in Dorchester, Massachusetts Bay, and that she was the daughter of one of the first immigrant families on *Mary and John*, in which case they had known each other since 1630 at least. They would have three children: Joshua II, born in 1638, Elias, born in 1643, and Elisha, born in 1646, all in Windsor, Connecticut.

The houses built on these lots were modest for a property of 115 acres, most of which was fertile land used to grow crops or manage cattle. A typical home was timber framed, with a minimum of foundation on bare earth, and with a sharply pitched roof to keep off the snow. It was small with two rooms downstairs, a parlor, and hall or kitchen, and a loft upstairs reached by a circular stair by the chimney. The ceilings were low and the windows small. The loft could be changed to two bedrooms. All was typical of early New England houses.

From the beginning Hartford, not Windsor, became the leading settlement in the Connecticut River Valley. This is because of the dominant figure of the Reverend Thomas Hooker, its founder, who led his large following there in 1636. Hooker had been born in Leicestershire in England in 1586, educated at Emmanuel College, Cambridge, and became a minister in the Church of England. In 1630 he was ordered to appear before the high commission for nonconformist preaching and fled to Holland to escape punishment. From there he immigrated to the Massachusetts Bay Colony in 1633 with some of his following. A dispute there with the Reverend John Cotton about Massachusetts's Puritan rigidity prompted the move to Hartford, Connecticut and the pastorship of the First Church in 1636. His major civic accomplishment was to draft the Fundamental Orders in 1639 under which Connecticut was long governed. Although never governor of the colony he was in many ways Connecticut's founding father. He remained pastor in Hartford to his death in 1647 at age 61. His chief assistant for the Connecticut years was the Reverend Samuel Stone, who had been born in Hertford, England, hence the name of the Connecticut capital city. Stone had been educated at Emmanuel as well and later had accompanied Captain Mason as chaplain on the Mystic Fort destruction.

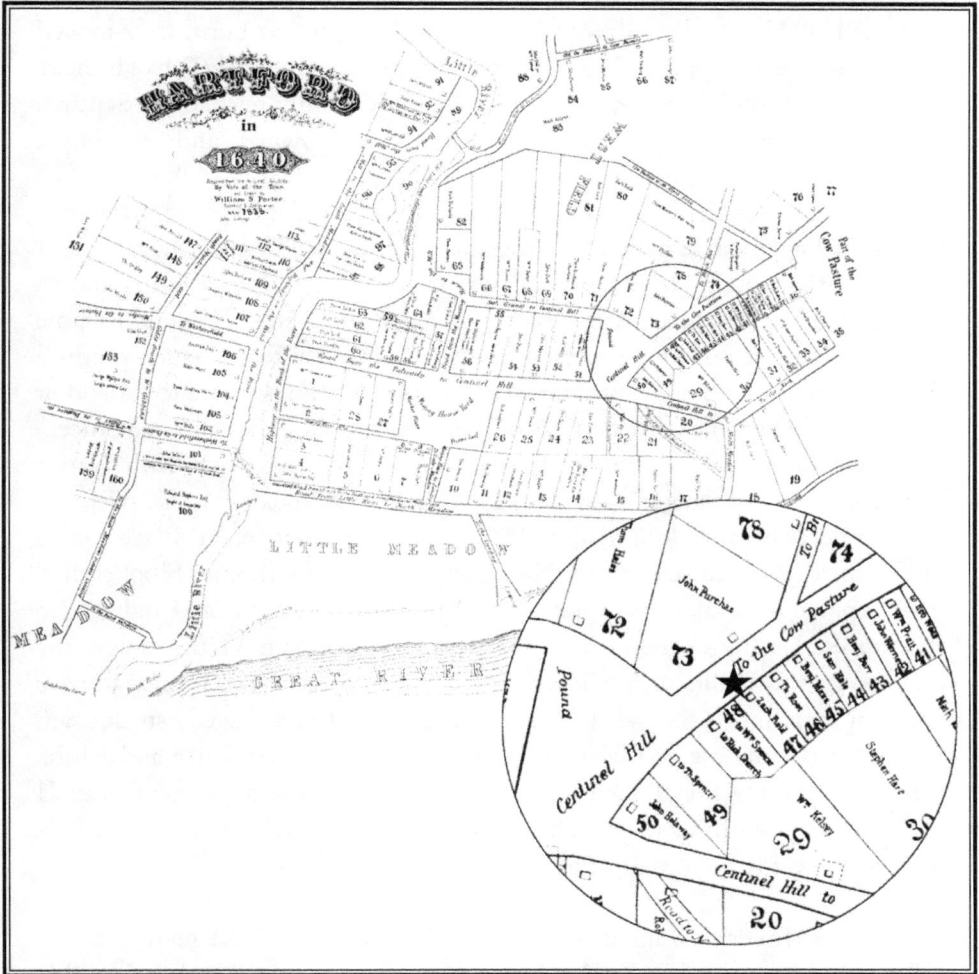

The map of Hartford, Connecticut, where Zechariah Field settled in 1636. His property is idenitfied with a star.

Zechariah Field, Hartford resident, who had been with Mason and Stone on this expedition, married Mary Stanley in 1641. They would have a family of five children. A girl named Mary, for her mother, was born in about 1643, followed by four sons: Zechariah, born about 1645; John, born about 1648; Samuel, born about 1651; and Joseph, born about 1658. It appears that the family remained in Hartford until 1659 when, after Joseph was born, they moved upriver to Northampton, Massachusetts, and then again in 1663 to Hatfield, Massachusetts. While still in Hartford the Field family resided on Sentinel Hill near the north end of Main Street. Field also owned land on what is known today as Asylum Street.

The decade of the 1640s was a different time in New England. Immigration from England had halted with the advent of the Civil War: King Charles I vs. the Parliament in 1642. Some Puritans actually returned to England to fight in the Parliamentary army. As the population of New England became stagnant, the price of food declined, and the farmers suffered. Much produce from the fertile riverbanks went uneaten. There was little pressure to expand or create new settlements. The families of Ancestor Field in Hartford and Ancestor Carter in Windsor were growing up in this time of peace with Native tribes. The greatest danger was from pestilence. A smallpox epidemic swept up the Connecticut River killing up to 90 percent of the Natives in villages south of Deerfield. Other diseases were killing settlers. In 1647 Thomas Hooker died in an "epidemic sickness". On July 15 that year Joshua Carter of Windsor also succumbed, leaving Catherine a widow with three children. Within a year, she married Arthur Williams, a fellow resident of Windsor, and continued to have children with him. Zebediah Williams was born in 1649. Tragedy stuck again for her in the middle of the night of May 10, 1653, when Elias and Elisha Carter died in the fire as their house burned to the ground. Joshua Carter II survived along with his mother, his stepfather and his half brother Zebediah. Joshua II was fifteen at that time.

During the 1650s, immigration from England and Scotland revived again. Oliver Cromwell ruled in England. The Puritans there were hearing favorable reports from New England of prosperity, to worship god as they wished. The population pressure grew along the Connecticut River pushing northward into Massachusetts with the founding of Northampton in 1659.

In 1658 Arthur and Catherine Williams sold their land in Windsor and moved to Northampton with sons Zebediah Williams, age 9, and Joshua Carter, age 20. Joshua took a house two lots away from them on Market Street. They had followed the founders of Northampton, Thomas Strong, David Wilton and Aaron Cooke, all from Windsor, who had paved the way. In 1661 the First Church of Northampton was established by the Reverend Eleazer Mather of the Boston clerical family of that name. Mather was married to Esther Warham, the daughter of Windsor minister Reverend John Warham. Founding members included Arthur and Catherine Williams. In 1659 Zechariah and Mary Field with their children also moved to Northampton from Hartford, a significant move for a family so well established in the history of that town.

With the death of the Reverend Thomas Hooker in 1647, a slow change began in theology practiced in Hooker's church and in those in Windsor and Wethersfield, and with it began a controversy. It concerned "the qualification for baptism, church membership, and the rights of the brotherhood."[7] This issue had begun to divide the three Connecticut settlements into two groups, those who favored baptism only for those who affirmed their faith in the Puritan doctrines of the church, as opposed to those who accepted baptism for all children. A so-called Half-Way Covenant was established as a compromise to permit infant baptism of children of non-members of the church, but that was never accepted by the most conservative establishment of the Puritan ministry.

In Hartford Zechariah and Mary Field made the decision to leave their church and their city in 1659 and with sixty other "dissident members" move north upriver to the new settlements of Northampton, Hatfield and Hadley, all in Massachusetts. "The most prominent and controlling cause which led to the settling of Hadley and Hatfield was, without doubt, the disagreement that arose in the churches that had been planted at Hartford, Wethersfield and Windsor, Connecticut."[8] Field cared more for free religious thought than for following set doctrine and in reality became as much a dissenter as were the Pilgrims of 1620, although he probably did not admit to that word. The real question became who would make theological decisions for the body of the church.

Rodney Field, a descendant states in the family genealogy, "Zechariah purchased in Northampton on the east side of the river a tract of property nine miles square, nearly twelve miles up and down the river. He himself settled in Northampton where he was involved in mercantile business and had a large

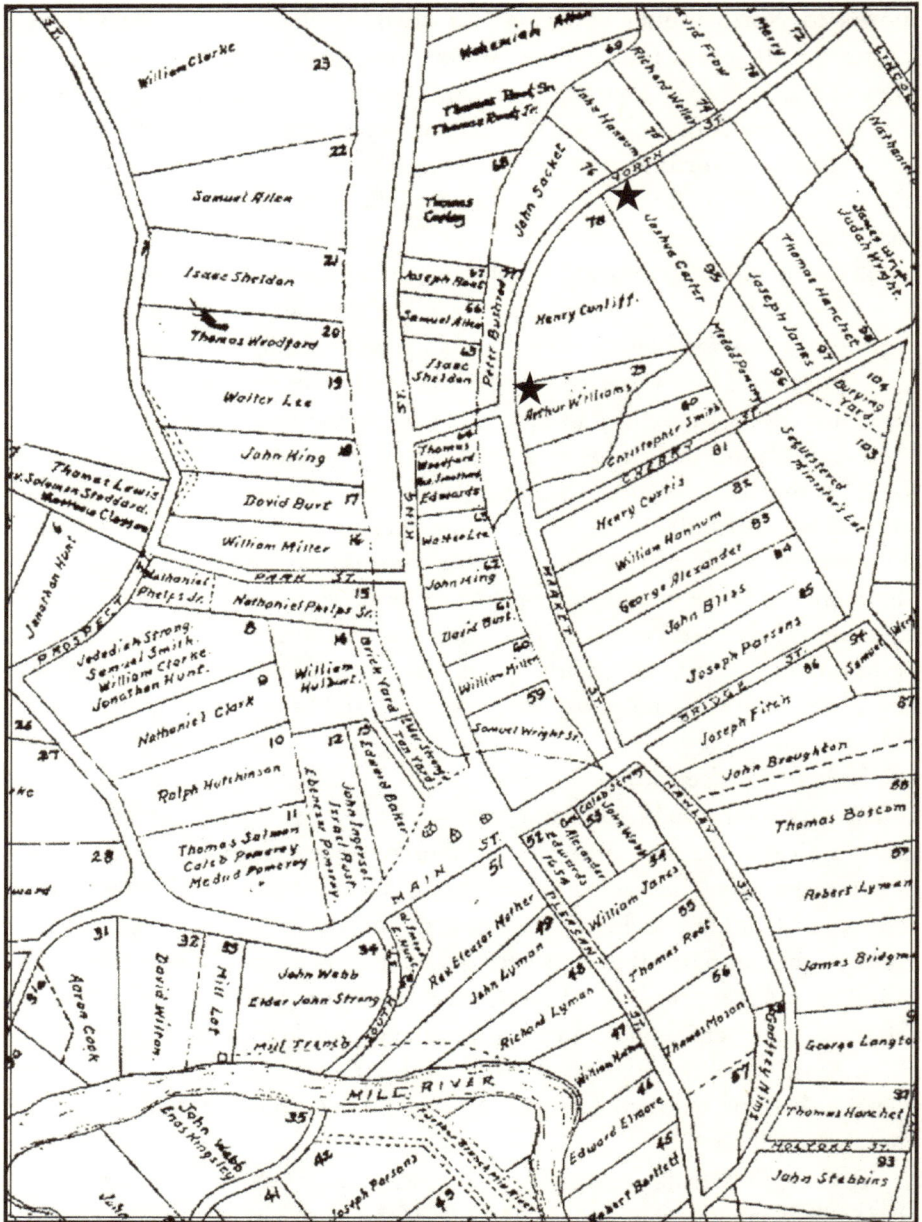

The map of Northampton, Massachusetts, where Joshua Carter II and his mother, Catherine Williams, located in 1658. Their properties were near each other and are identified on the map with stars.

trade with the Indians."[9] Then in 1661 two years later, "he was one of the twenty-five persons to settle in what is now Hatfield." Since moving to this area the Field and the Carter families were located reasonably near each other and came to know each other.

Thus it was that on October 6, 1663, Joshua Carter II of Northampton, age 25, married Mary Field, age 20, daughter of Zechariah and Mary Field of Hatfield. A son was born to them in 1665 in Northampton and named Samuel likely after Mary's younger brother, Samuel Field.

On June 30, 1666 Zechariah Field died in Hatfield, Massachusetts, the town of which he was a founder. He was about 70 years old. The immigrant from Yorkshire had lived in Dorchester, in Hartford, and finally in Northampton and Hatfield. He was mostly associated with Hartford from where he fought the Pequot tribe and was a congregant of the notable Reverend Thomas Hooker. He was buried at Soldiers Field in Hartford. Zechariah Field's wife, Mary, died in about 1670. Of their five children, Mary married Joshua Carter II, as mentioned, and their son John married Mary Edwards. The families of both these brothers-in-law would be living in Deerfield, Massachusetts on the fateful night of February 29, 1704.

In 1668 while still in Northampton, Joshua and Mary Carter bore a second son whom they named Joshua III. After Deerfield was founded in 1670 they began to look north to the fertile plain and meadow on the Deerfield River that had so attracted Native tribes for so many centuries. In 1672 they moved, and two years later Joshua became a constable of the community. For a very short time all seemed well.

There had been thirty-eight years of relatively peaceful relations between the English settlers and the various Native tribes of New England when a war broke out in 1675. It is known today as King Philip's War. For more than a year all of New England was in turmoil. The settlers called it a rebellion against authority and control, which they believed came from God.

Philip was a Native, the Wampanoag tribe leader, son of Massasoit, who greeted the Pilgrims in 1621. The English leader was Josiah Winslow, governor of the Plymouth Colony (still separate from Massachusetts Bay). Historian Nathaniel Philbrick summarized the conflict:

> King Philip's War lasted only fourteen months, but it changed the face of New England. After fifty-five years of peace, the lives of Native and English peoples had become so intimately intertwined that when

fighting broke out, many of the region's Indians found themselves, in the words of a contemporary chronicler, "in a kind of maze, not knowing what to do." Some Indians chose to support Philip; others joined the colonial forces; still others attempted to stay out of the conflict altogether. Violence quickly spread until the entire region became a terrifying war zone. A third of the hundred or so towns in New England were burned and abandoned. There was even a proposal to build a barricade around the core settlements of Massachusetts and surrender the towns outside the perimeter to Philip and his allies.

The colonial forces ultimately triumphed, but at a horrifying cost. There were approximately seventy thousand people in New England at the outbreak of hostilities. By the end of the war, somewhere in the neighborhood of five thousand were dead, with more than three-quarters of those losses suffered by the Native Americans. In terms of percentage of population killed, King Philip's War was more than twice as bloody as the American Civil War and at least seven times more lethal than the American Revolution.[10]

The frontier of Massachusetts, which included the Connecticut River Valley, erupted into violence on August 2, 1675, with an attack by the Nipmuck tribe on the town of Brookfield, which lay between Boston and the Connecticut River in an isolated wilderness area. The town's twenty houses were burned to the ground. For two days, eighty people, mostly women and children, were besieged in one house before a relief party of troopers arrived from Boston and the Indians dispersed.

From Brookfield, the Nipmucks moved on to Lancaster and killed eight English. Near the end of the month the settlers held a council of war in Hatfield on the Connecticut River, which resulted in a force of one hundred English being sent out to protect the villages along the river as the war quickly spread up and down the valley. The battle of South Deerfield resulted in nine English and twenty-six Indian deaths. In September, the northernmost town of Northfield was completely evacuated after twenty-one English had been slaughtered. By mid-September, the only question was Where will the Nipmucks attack next? The question was soon answered in what was to be the bloodiest battle of the war: the battle of Bloody Brook.

On September 18, the town of Deerfield, which had been settled only five years earlier, was being evacuated because it was in a relatively isolated location. The party of seventy-nine residents, led by Captain Thomas Lathrop and a company of about fifty soldiers, had reached a stream crossing about a half dozen miles south of Deerfield; the soldiers had put their guns in carts to gather ripe autumn grapes when they were ambushed by the Nipmucks. Almost all of the New England soldiers died in the attack, along with fourteen men from Deerfield—close to half of the adult males. A third of the families lost their fathers, including both of Catherine Carter William's sons: Joshua Carter II, husband of Mary Field Carter and father of ten-year-old Samuel Carter, and Joshua's half-brother, Zedediah Williams. During this battle the water in the brook turned red, giving the name Bloody Brook to the encounter.* Three days later, Deerfield was completely emptied of English settlers; by the following spring, the Indians were planting corn in the fields as they had for decades in the past. Deerfield was one of the few towns that the Natives regained in the fourteen-month war. The others that were attacked and raided were successfully defended. The residents of nearby Hatfield, Hadley, and Northampton stayed put.

King Philip's War officially ended with the sachem's death in 1676. By late spring that year the English had gained the initiative. The Mohawk tribe from the Hudson River region, never friendly with the New England Natives, turned against them and began to support the English. The climax of the many tragedies occurred when two to three hundred Natives were killed or drowned in a surprise attack in May on the shore of the Connecticut River. New England's most destructive war ever was over, although ambushes did continue from time to time, especially on the frontier towns. When settlers tried to reoccupy Deerfield in 1677, they were repulsed. It was not until early in 1682 that English settlers returned to Deerfield to stay. Three-fifths of these families came from Northampton, Hadley, and Hatfield to the south. Some of these were survivors of the earlier (1670) settlement such as the Carter and Field families. In 1690, Samuel Carter, then twenty-five years old, son of the deceased Joshua Carter II and his wife Mary, was married in Deerfield to Mercy Brooks, daughter of William and Mary Brooks, of Springfield, Massachusetts, where Mercy had been born in 1661.

A History of Deerfield

Before it was first occupied by English settlers in 1670, Deerfield had been a home for Native tribes for hundreds of years. Men hunted and fished, women

---

*   Bloody Brook flows into the Connecticut River south of South Deerfield, Massachusetts.

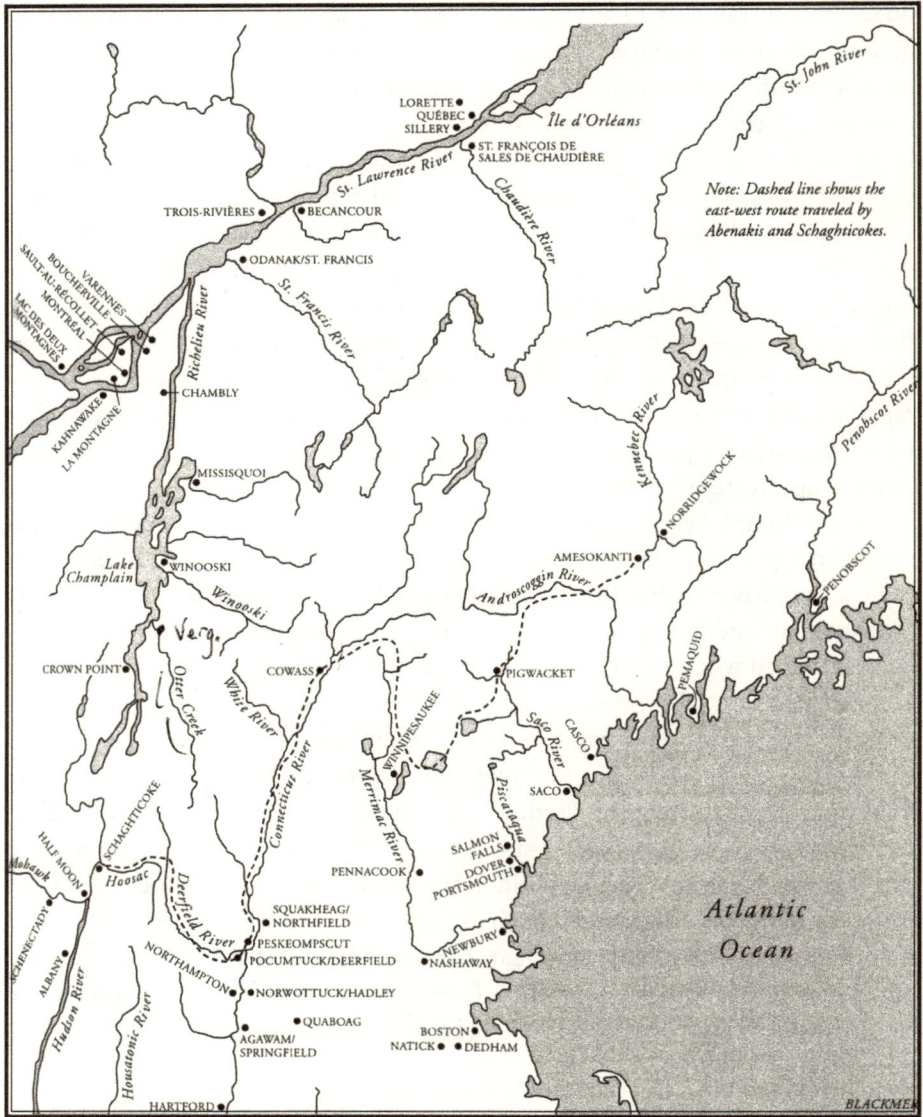

A map from 1660 to 1725 showing that Pocumtuck-Deerfield was at an intersection of Native trading throughout the Northeast from 1600. Pocumtuck village had five hundred to one thousand residents at that time. Cowass on the Connecticut River is called Newbury today.

gathered food and cared for homes. Its location on both sides of the Deerfield River, only a few miles before it flows into the Connecticut River, was fertile flat land ideal for planting corn and rich grassland that attracted game. By 1600, the village could have had five hundred to one thousand Native residents. Different tribes lived along the Connecticut River, but they were generally friendly, intermarried, traded with each other, and spoke similar languages.

Because of its geographic location Deerfield was in a unique position. It was an ancient crossroads. What the English later called a frontier town was in fact an intersection in the midst of New England for Native tribes traveling from the Hudson River on the west to Maine and Cape Cod on the east, and from Long Island Sound on the south to the Saint Lawrence Valley in Canada on the north. This was the underlying reason for the terrible conflicts that occurred in Deerfield from the 1670s to the 1760s, a period of almost one hundred years. The English population explosion in New England, the many Native tribes that occupied the area, and the French occupation of the St. Lawrence Valley came together in clashes that killed hundreds of each group. Deerfield had more than its share of these.

Because New England and Lower Canada were hilly and heavily wooded lands, travel throughout could only occur on the several rivers, and Deerfield was at the junction of two important ones: the Connecticut to the north and south, and the Deerfield to the west. From the Connecticut to the north, Natives could go up the White River across the Green Mountains and down the Winooski to Lake Champlain, then down the Richelieu to the St. Lawrence. From further north on the Connecticut they could connect with a short portage to the Merrimack and then down to Maine and northern Massachusetts. From the Deerfield River they could travel west to connect with a short portage to the Hoosac River, which flows into the Hudson north of Albany. The map shows how critical an intersection the site of Deerfield was and how readily it could be reached by the Natives and by the French from Montreal in the wars to come (see map).

Two years after Deerfield had been abandoned by its English settlers during King Philip's War, some of them attempted to return in 1675 but were unsuccessful. Fighting continued throughout parts of New England. It was not until the spring of 1682 that a real community with homes could be established again. It included eighteen of the original settler families. The new group also included persons of more prominence and wealth, who became the town

leaders. Two brothers, Thomas and Jonathan Wells from nearby Hadley, became military leaders. A church was established, managed by laymen in one of
the homes. In 1686, the community leaders invited a twenty-two-year-old
graduate of Harvard College, John Williams, to be their minister. He accepted
the task—which two others had declined—and would become a great success.
His wife, Eunice Mather from Northampton, was the daughter of a Reverend
Eleazer Mather of Northampton and a niece of the notable Reverend Increase
Mather of Boston, the leading clergyman in the Massachusetts Bay Colony.
This connection would help Deerfield in its great time of trial.

The Congregational Church established there was much like all the others
in the colony and much like the churches in East Anglia. "Ordered Liberty"
was emphasized and preached from the pulpit. The Puritan concepts of Grace
and The Word as preached by the minister as the Word of God were accepted
by the congregation. They settled in Deerfield in search of land, not because of
church order. Like in every church in Massachusetts, non-members as well as
members were required by law to attend Sunday service. Punishments were
meted out for failure to be present. Ceremony was minimal. The celebration of
Christmas was forbidden in Massachusetts on pain of five shillings. In confor-
mity to the Half-Way Covenant, baptism was given to most children and full
membership to most adults, except for those whose lives were morally scandal-
ous in the opinion of the town leaders. The minister—addressed as Minister
Williams—was a town leader in spite of his young age. He was the contact
with Boston if help was needed, as it often was. His salary was sixty pounds per
year, on a par with those in Northampton and Hadley. Like several other Puritan ministers, he was a slave owner whose African Americans performed
household tasks.

Soon after Mr. Williams arrived in Deerfield, fighting with the Natives
broke out again. This time it was the Abenaki tribe from the St. Lawrence Valley in Canada and from eastern Maine who raided Northfield in the summer
of 1688. They had come south from Canada on the established route up the
Richelieu River, Lake Champlain, the Winooski River, and across the divide to
the Connecticut River down to Northfield. In 1690, Northfield was abandoned
and Deerfield became the most vulnerable town. When the English and the
French went to war again in Europe in 1689—the so-called Nine Years War or
King William's War by the French—the attacks in New England were stepped
up, and the Natives were joined and often led by the French who were living in
New France along the St. Lawrence River. More about that will follow later.

To defend themselves, Deerfield residents for the first time in 1690 constructed a stockade that encircled the ten houses in the center of the village. Residents living in houses outside the stockade were expected to move inside during times of extreme danger. Much to their annoyance, the settlers watched an almost constant stream of Native peoples use their town as a crossroads. Most of these, but not all, were peaceful.

Conditions worsened in 1690, the year the Carters married. Troops arriving from the Connecticut Colony to protect Deerfield brought with them a "sickness" that had ravaged the lower river valley the year before. Some died, many were ailing, and most residents were so fearful of the sickness that fields were not plowed or tended properly. Food became scarce. It seemed like the biblical plague had come to Deerfield. Thomas Wells, town leader, died in 1691; caterpillars devoured the corn crop in 1692; then in June 1693 Indians killed three or four residents and captured another; in 1694 a large force made an assault but were beaten off, Mr. Williams barely escaping from a party lying in ambush; in 1695 and 1696, Natives returned to ambush anyone who went outside the stockade. During all this time, twelve Deerfield residents had been killed and five captured. Some also left, although doing so was against the law of Massachusetts, which penalized them with the loss of their land. Despite this law, nine families left in the fifteen years from 1689 to 1704. With the end of the war in Europe in 1697, conditions in Deerfield remained relatively safe, and a degree of prosperity followed. The pastor, Mr. Williams, and his wife continued to have children; ten were born in their fifteen years of marriage, eight of whom survived childhood, which was a good average in that era.

The respite was short, however, as in 1702, only five years after peace in Europe, the English and French went to war again. This time it was called "The War of the Spanish Succession" or Queen Anne's War by the French. And this time it would last for ten years! Deerfield was again an endangered frontier town. By the end of 1703 it contained about fifty families and 260 to 270 residents, only slightly more than in 1688. During that interval the Carter family had substantially changed.

The Carters of Deerfield

Following their marriage in December 1690, Samuel and Mercy Carter followed the custom of many Puritan families by having children quickly and often. Samuel Jr. and Mercy, born in 1692 and 1693, were named for their

The Carter family cottage with its gambrel roof is today the wing of the Old Manse in Deerfield, Massachusetts, owned by Deerfield Academy. The photograph of the wing was taken by Adaline Havemeyer in 2012.

parents in Puritan tradition. Then John was born in 1695, Ebenezer in 1697, Thomas in 1699, and Marah in 1701. While delivering Marah on January 22nd that year, Mercy Carter died in childbirth. Samuel was married again later that year to Hannah Weller; a son, Joseph, was born in May of 1702 and a daughter, Hannah, in July of 1703. The family status of Samuel and Hannah at the beginning of 1704 was four boys, three girls, and one deceased infant— eight children with two wives in an interval of thirteen years. The eldest, Samuel Jr., was eleven years old.

During much if not all of that time, two other families who were related to the Carters were in Deerfield as well. They were Nathaniel and Mary Brooks, brother and sister-in-law of Mercy Carter, and John and Mary Field. John was an uncle of Samuel Carter. The Carters lived in a separate house within the stockade, and the Brooks and Field families lived in houses outside the enclosure. They all realized that the time was particularly perilous with the start of the new war in Europe, but they had survived Native attacks and ambushes several times before and were prepared to face them again. What they did not appreciate and could not predict was the new role to be played by France.

New France

The St. Lawrence watershed begins in the lakes of Minnesota and flows eastward through the five Great Lakes until it reaches the river of that name where it heads northeast to the Atlantic Ocean between Newfoundland and Nova Scotia. It is one of the largest watersheds on the North American continent. It connects through the Chicago River to the Mississippi-Missouri watershed, which flows south to the Gulf of Mexico at New Orleans, Louisiana. King Louis XIV of France, the Sun King, wanted all this land and its water routes for his country. It was to be known as the colony of New France.

Long before the time of the Sun King, in 1534 a French navigator and explorer, Jacques Cartier, discovered the mouth of the St. Lawrence River in eastern Canada and sailed upriver—to sites that would later be Quebec and Montreal—where he discovered Indian villages. He made three voyages there over an eight-year period but never established a lasting settlement. It was only forty years or so after Columbus's voyages to the Caribbean. Explorers were searching for the Orient and for gold then; they were not looking to establish settlements in cold climates. That would come later. But France did claim what Cartier had seen on his voyages.

In the next century, in 1603, another French explorer, Samuel de Champlain, set forth for the new world with the formation of settlements in mind. A year later he established a small one called Port Royal on the western side of Nova Scotia. Four years later, on another voyage in 1608, he established the first permanent French settlement on the north bank of the mighty St. Lawrence River, called Quebec. On that same trip he sailed upriver and then up a major tributary to discover a large lake that he named after himself: Lake Champlain. He returned to France but came back again many times to explore further west all the way to Lake Ontario, making friends with many different Indian tribes along the river. He learned very early that he had uncovered a new form of gold. If he would give the Natives gunpowder, they would trade beaver skins, of which there seemed an endless supply the further west he went. And the Europeans were enamored with fur from beavers. This became the economic engine that would develop New France. Unfortunately for the French, by 1624 the Dutch in New Netherland had discovered this fact as well. There was competition for the fur trade, and the Natives found out how to take advantage of that. The Dutch and later the English favored trade with the Iroquois Five Nations, and the French favored the many St. Lawrence tribes, resulting in a war between them throughout all of the seventeenth century. After thousands of Natives had been killed, the Great Peace of Montreal was signed in 1701, with the Iroquois conceding the land west of Montreal to the French and their Indian allies. The French needed these allies to hold the upper country and so contain the British colonies on the Atlantic seaboard. The Indian wars corresponded in time with the European wars, usually England against France and Spain, all of which made life for peaceful Puritan settlers in Massachusetts very difficult, particularly in a frontier town such as Deerfield.

There was an inherent conflict between the French and Spanish on the one hand and the English Puritans on the other. Although all were Christian nations in the seventeenth century, their beliefs, customs, and practices, which greatly affected the lives of the people, were entirely different. In the case of New France against New England it was Roman Catholic against conservative Protestantism, and wars were fought in Europe almost constantly between the two. This had a reaction in the New World as well, as we shall see. To sum up, in New France emphasis was placed on fur trading and converting Natives to

Roman Catholicism, whereas in New England the emphasis was on settlements, population growth, and economic prosperity.

Armand Jean du Plessis, Cardinal de Richelieu, was a French statesman and minister of France under Louis XIII from 1624 until his death in 1642. From about 1630, as chief minister he was in complete control of the government of his country. His domestic policy was to strengthen the central power against the nobility and to persecute the Huguenots, even though the Edict of Nantes, which protected them, was still in effect. His foreign policy was to build colonies abroad and particularly in North America. It was Richelieu who in the 1620s had established "New France" in Canada as a Roman-Catholic colony. It was controlled by him directly from Paris. He gave large land holdings along the St. Lawrence River to French Nobles called *seigneurs* who agreed to permanently live there. In 1642 a village on Montreal Island, called Ville Marie de Montreal, was one of these *seigneuries*. In spite of this, New France never attracted the numbers of settlers that came to New England in the same period. After Richelieu's death, the river connecting Lake Champlain to the St. Lawrence River was named after him. It was the easiest route from Canada to the back door of New England at Deerfield. It also became the attack route for warring parties from Canada, and much later a logging route to mills established along the shores of Lake Champlain such as in Vergennes. In 1701, King Louis XIV informed his governor in Canada that he intended to use New France, by then a Royal colony, as a military barrier for blocking English access to the interior of North America. With royal instruction and with the beginning of the War of Spanish Succession the following year, the new governor, Philippe de Rigaud de Vaudreuil, born in Quebec but descended from an old French noble family, could plan an aggressive strike against the English at its most vulnerable place: Deerfield, Massachusetts.

War Plans

Governor Vaudreuil recognized that the attack party must consist of both French Canadian officers and soldiers and Native tribes friendly to them. Without Native support he knew that New France could not be sustained as a colony. Furthermore, because of tribal jealousy, he also knew that warriors from five major tribes must take part in the effort. They were the Abenakis, who had driven back the English frontier in Maine, and tribes from the St. Lawrence villages of Lorette, La Montagne, Sault-au-Récollet, Kahnawake, and Odanak. All these villages were also sites of Christian missions maintained by French priests. About two hundred warriors joined the party.

The French contingent of fifty officers and men was to be led by thirty-five-year-old Lieutenant Jean-Baptiste Hertel de Rouville. He and ten other officers were Canadian-born members of the French nobility whose families had emigrated with grants from Richelieu. Hertel, the commander, came from the military nobility, as did seven of his brothers. The other family of military officers was the Bouchers from Montreal. This officer leadership of both the French and Natives was as competent as could be found for planning and executing a raid on a village over three hundred miles away. If they could get there without warning, they could hardly fail to overwhelm the settlers of Deerfield. They had been trained and hardened by a half century of struggle with the Five Nations of the Iroquois League—whose alliance with the English had only recently ended with the Montreal peace treaty in 1701.

The assembly point chosen by Hertel for the expedition was the town of Chambly on the Richelieu River south and east of Montreal. It was conveniently near the villages of all the participants and was the seat of Hertel's father. During the autumn of 1703, the various tribes began to gather at Chambly; by the end of the year, close to two hundred warriors huddled around the fires with the fifty Canadians preparing to march south.

There had been warnings in 1703 that another raid on Deerfield would take place. They were taken seriously by Massachusetts officials and town residents. In May, the English governor of New York had learned from spies that a party of French and Indians had gathered near Montreal, but as the summer came and went, nothing happened. The governor of Connecticut was cautious and skeptical, believing that French raiders would come from Quebec, four hundred miles away (and not Montreal, only 280 miles away), thus giving plenty of warning. In August, three Mohawks had returned from Canada with news that three hundred Indians with some French would come to New England. To defend their homes Deerfield residents looked to local militia. Every fit man in the town from age sixteen to sixty, about seventy in all, was charged with its defense. They had practiced maneuvering and firing as in a European pitched battle, which would be of no use against an Indian attack. Then on October 8, Natives ambushed two Deerfield men, Zebediah Williams (no relation to John Williams) and his half-brother John Nims, as they watched over animals pastured outside the stockade. Both were captured and taken it Canada, where Williams died in captivity and Nims escaped. The two were cousins of Samuel Carter.

Meanwhile at Chambly, the raid against the Connecticut River Valley had been delayed when English ships were spotted near the entrance of the St. Lawrence River. This persuaded the Abenakis in the group to go to Maine to protect their interests in their homeland. They remained there until the fall. The French force at Chambly were worried about the peace treaty with the Iroquois nation. If they went south, leaving Montreal unprotected, would the Iroquois attack the city? Finally, Governor Vaudreuil received a letter from France urging that the planned attack on Deerfield go ahead, with the mission to spread as much terror along the New England frontier as possible in hopes that the English would not try to invade New France. That was its intent and its goal. By January 1704, Lieutenant Hertel began to move out with the largest expedition ever assembled on the American continent up to that time—250 men strong to travel 280 miles and return on foot and by canoe. It was also the first expedition of any size that was clearly led by the French, not the Indians who would not attempt to capture and destroy an entire fortified town.

Late in January more warnings began to arrive that an expedition was on the march. The Massachusetts governor warned his commanders along the Connecticut River that three hundred Indians were on the move. Soldiers were sent to garrison Deerfield, arriving there on February 25. By then the expedition had reached the Connecticut River at Cowass (today Newport, Vermont) and was joined by the Pennacock tribe with fifty more men. They had successfully crossed the Green Mountains in the dead of winter, having gone up Lake Champlain, up the Winooski River, and down the Wells River to the Connecticut River. From there, the leg of the journey to Deerfield was all downhill.*

To some degree, all the false alarms gave Deerfield a false sense of security. Snow was deep in February and some were complacent, thinking an attack would not come in mid-winter and at night. It is doubtful that any residents knew that when they arose the next day it would be Leap Year, February 29, 1704. It would be a day that none would ever forget.

---

* The course of the Winooski River was established before the formation of the Green Mountains. The river rises east of these mountains and cuts through them, passing by Montpelier on its way to Lake Champlain near Burlington, Vermont. It is ninety miles long.

The Assault

The expedition had arrived north of Deerfield the previous day. They spent a night without fires camped on Petty Plain, across the Deerfield River about two miles north of town. Well before dawn they crossed the river and took up positions in the meadows north of the village. A scouting party had found the watchman asleep at the stockade. Two hours before dawn, Lieutenant Hertel ordered the attack to begin. It was a complete surprise to all the residents, most of whom were asleep.

A three-foot blanket of snow covered the meadows as a volunteer Native with snowshoes silently approached the stockade near the north gate, easily walked up the snow bank against the wall, and slipped over to unlock the gate from the inside. The first part of the raiding party through the gate went to the easternmost house, which was owned by the Carter family. Other parts went in other directions to reach all of the houses within the enclosure. There was competition among the various groups of raiders to see who would get more high-value captives for later ransom. Twenty Indians representing four different tribes attacked the home of Reverend Williams and his large family. He was seized, disarmed, and held in captivity, as was his wife. Of the children, two young ones were killed, together with the female slave, and the rest captured. They were allowed to dress while in the house but were then removed to the town meetinghouse; their home was then torched. Residents of other houses suffered a similar fate.

On the eastern side of the compound a group of Kahnawake Mohawks overwhelmed the occupants of the Carter house. Young five-year-old Thomas Carter was killed in the raid. The rest of the children were captured, as was their mother Hannah. There is a question about Samuel, the father of the family. What is certain is that Samuel was neither killed nor captured that night. The authors of *Captors and Captives* state on page 115 that "only Samuel Carter managed to escape in the ensuing confusion." It is true that many of the men, who were able to get dressed and were armed, knew they had no chance against their attackers and went to get help, some as far as Hatfield. Possibly Samuel Carter was one of those. Other sources said:

> Samuel Carter had been delayed while taking care of business at a distance too far for him to return to Deerfield on the same day. When he returned to Deerfield, he discovered that he had lost his entire family of eight people. It was somewhat of a miracle that, within the ruins

Sheldons

2K
4C 3E
SHELDON

E. Brooks 3E

D. Hoyt Sen 7C 2E
J. Stebbins 7C

1K
7C 1E
CARTER

B
1K
14*E
B. STEBBINS

MEETING
HOUSE

1K
7C
FRENCH

N. Belden

B
3K
8C 1E
WILLIAMS

J. Stoddard

B
1K
2C 1E
J. HAWKS SEN

B
2K
2C 1E
CATLIN

Allisons 2E
S. Smead 4K 1E
J. Hawks Jr. 6K
Stevens 1K 1C
Hurst 7C
Field 1K 3C 1E

B
3K
1C 2E
FRARY

1K
3C
HINSDALE

B
1C
5E
RICHARDS
Munn 3E

Richardses

G. Nims

B
7K
4C 1E
NIMS

B
N. BROOKS

J. BROOKS

E. SMEAD

MAP KEY

B	Indicates house that was burned
K	Number killed at given location
C	Number captured at given location
E	Number escaped at given location
———	Approximate location of the palisade
·······▶	Probable direction of Native raiders
·······▶	Escape routes of residents

J. WELLS

NOTES
- Not to scale
- Names in italics indicate likely locations of people living in temporary shelters

BLACKMER

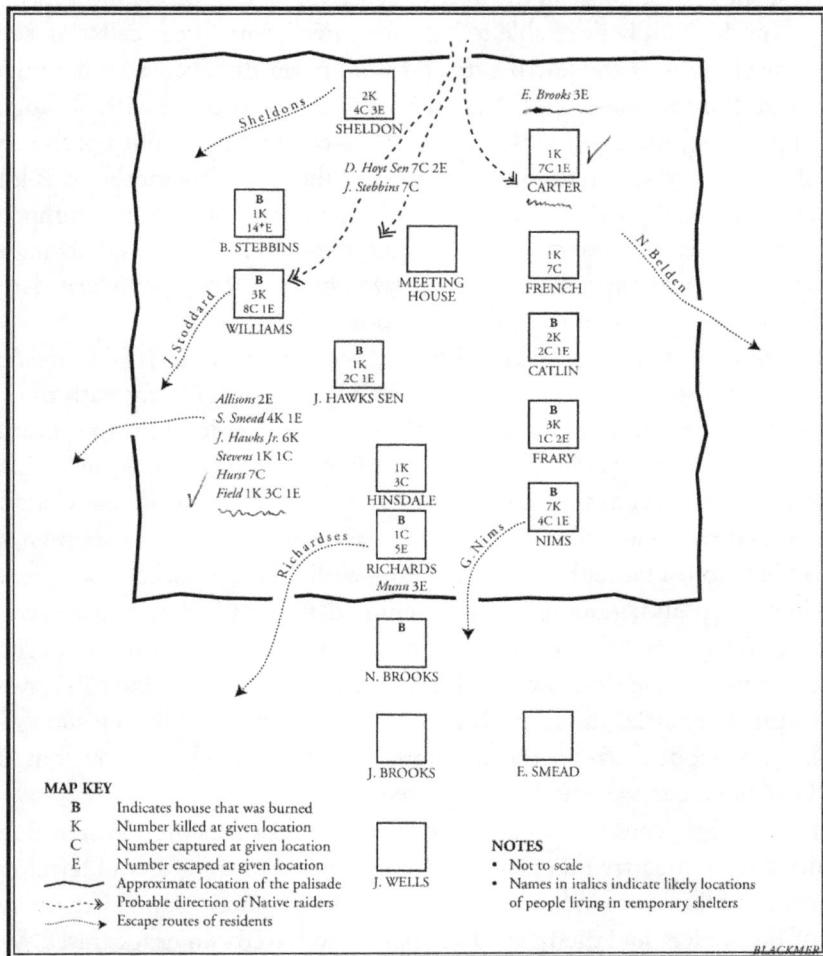

Note the cabin of Carter within the compound. Those of N. Brooks and John and Mary Field were outside. The Carter cabin was not burned down and survives today. Williams was the minister of the community.

of his village, his house had somehow been left standing and still stands today. Inside the house he discovered the body of his five-year-old son, Thomas Carter, on the stairway. He also discovered dead cattle, bullet marks, and general disorder. [11]

Near the Carter house in the northeast section of the compound, Ebenezer Brooks and his family were able to hide for three hours in the cellar of a temporary dwelling near the north gate and were never discovered by the raiders. They were the fortunate ones. Nathaniel and Mary Brooks, with a daughter Mary, age seven, and a son William, age six, lived in a house south of the compound. All four were captured in the raid and the children's mother was killed on the march back to Canada. John Field's house was outside the compound on the west side. John escaped while fleeing to get help from neighboring militia, but Mary was captured with their two children John and Mary. Samuel Field was killed later that day in the Meadows Fight.

It is thought that the raid lasted from three to three and a half hours. After assaulting all the houses, they started burning them, beginning with ones on the south and working north. The captives were all herded into the meeting-house while the raiders killed all the cattle, hogs, and sheep they could find to create as much terror as they could. These were their orders from the Canadian governor. At this point the English militia appeared. Thirty to forty men who had ridden from Hatfield and Hadley to Deerfield on horseback were joined with local men and, gaining strength, entered the south gate and forced the raiders to retreat. But the damage had been done and the expedition began to withdraw, taking their one hundred and eleven captives with them. There was never a pitched battle. The English were handicapped by not having snowshoes for the three-foot drifts in the meadow. The stockade was cleared but they could not pursue those who had destroyed Deerfield.

The English counterattack had caused Hertel's expedition some losses. Twenty-two of the fifty French had suffered injuries, among them Hertel himself, who had been wounded in an arm. English sources claim that thirty to fifty of the raiders had died, but that appears to have been exaggerated. With regard to the Deerfield residents, thirty-eight died in town, at least fifteen killed by fire in their houses. Another nine were killed in the fight on the Meadows; two from Deerfield and seven from other river towns who had come to help. One hundred and eleven captives were taken, mostly women and older children who were viewed as adoptees into the Native communities in Canada. Many of the youngest children perished on the return march.

The assault was a tactical victory for Governor Vaudreuil. By deploying fewer than fifty Frenchmen he rallied Native support and spread fear throughout New England. The colonies there had to mobilize almost two thousand men under arms during the summer of 1704 from Deerfield in the west to Wells, Maine, in the east. Meanwhile, the War of Spanish Succession, which had begun in 1702 in Europe, would last until 1712. Deerfield would recover slowly, but did experience ambushes again in 1708, 1709, and 1712—although nothing of the magnitude of the nightmare on February 29, 1704.

The Retreat to Canada: Twenty-Five Days of Torture

Although the destruction of Deerfield was an important victory for the French and their Native partners, the return home threatened to deprive them of the spoils of victory: the one hundred and eleven English captives, mostly women and older children, whom the Natives intended to ransom for money or, if that was not possible, to wed and adopt into their tribes. The French interest in these people was to educate and convert them into the Roman Catholic faith, thereby increasing the number of settlers in the St. Lawrence Valley. However it was still mid-winter along the route home, and the captives were not well protected from harsh conditions. Some of the women were weak, having never made a forced march, and many of the children were too small to keep up. Getting them back alive was a large problem. Only eighty-nine of them eventually reached Canada. Those who fell behind on the journey were killed by the Natives. A couple of males tried to escape but were recaptured, tortured, and burned to death at the stake. After this no one again tried to escape.

Of the seven members of the Carter family only four would reach Canada alive: sons Samuel Jr., John, and Ebenezer; and daughter Mercy. The mother, Hannah, age twenty-nine, was killed in the march on the third day, after an eighteen-mile trek in the snow. Having already lost two daughters, she gave up and was slain by her captor. Stepdaughter Marah, three years old, and daughter Hannah, only seven months old, had been killed the day before.

Nathaniel Brooks and his two children survived the march to Canada. Several years later he was ransomed and returned to Deerfield. His daughter Mary, it is thought, remarried in Canada as did John and Mercy Carter. The fate of his son William is not known.

The most prominent captive, the minister, John Williams, was treated bet-

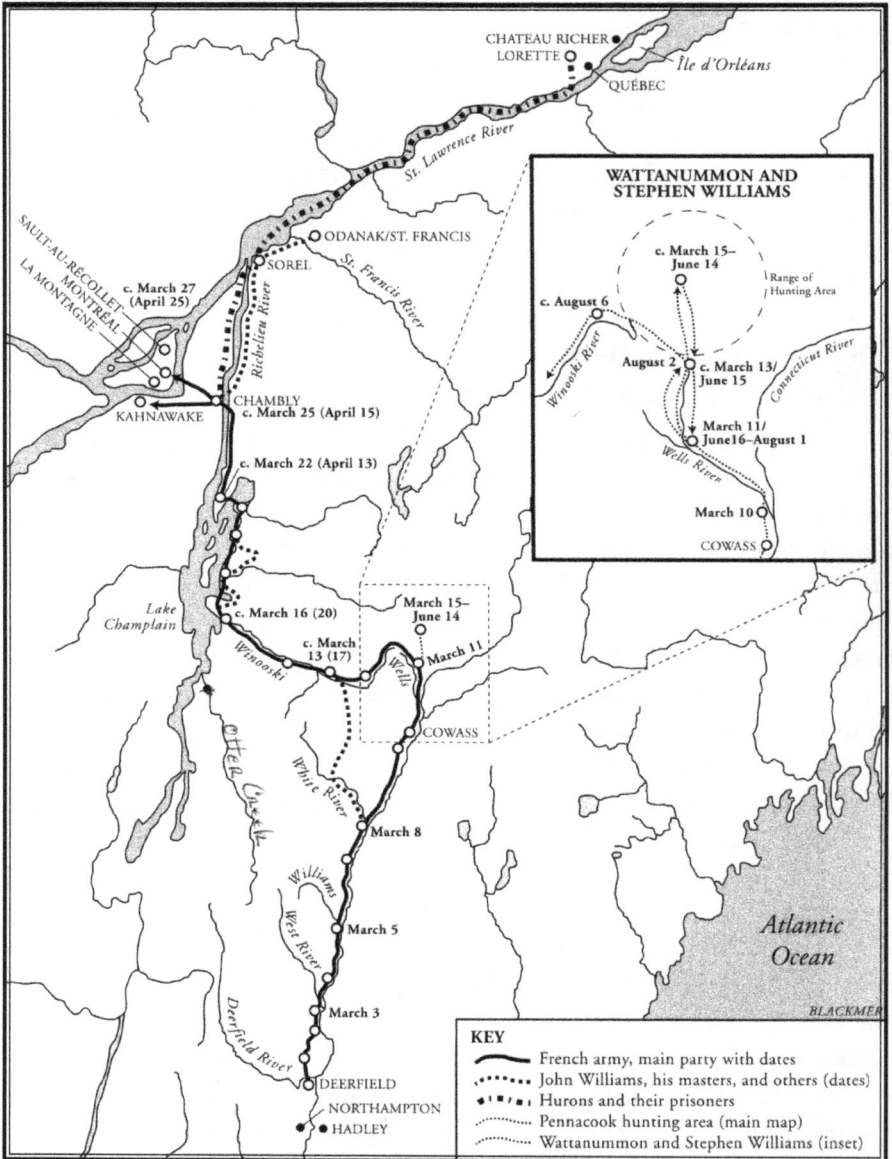

The route of the retreat from Deerfield, above, was the same as that of the advance from Chambly prior to the February 29 raid.

ter than many, although he had lost his wife on the second day. Eunice had delivered seven children, was thirty-nine years old, and had delivered her last child only six weeks before the attack. In her weakened condition she could not keep up. Separated from her husband, she asked to be released. With her captor she wandered into the woods and fell into a stream, where her captor ended her life with a blow of his hatchet. John Williams's captors, two Natives from the Abenaki tribe, took him all the way to Odanak on the St. Lawrence River where their fort was located. He would return to Deerfield two and a half years later. Four of the Williams family would also return to New England. One daughter, named Eunice for her mother, remained in Kahnawake, joined the Roman Catholic Church, married a Native, and with him had Roman Catholic children. She would visit her father from time to time. More of a Puritan than ever, he struggled greatly with her conversion.

The route back to Canada was the same for all except one, Stephen Williams, John's son. Most returned as they came to Chambly: on the Richelieu River. Leaving Deerfield on March 2, they arrived on March 25. Stephen with his captor remained for three months, hunting for game in the Connecticut River Valley north of Cowass.

A New Life for the Carters as Chartiers

Almost all the French and Indian raids in New England during the late seventeenth and early eighteenth centuries involved the taking of captives, the families of whom were not kept together. Some were taken to French homes in Canada, others to Native villages. Some, particularly men, were later exchanged for Frenchmen held by the English; others were ransomed and returned home after a period. Some, particularly women, were purchased from their Native captors by the French, who outdid the Natives in their desire and success in converting and adopting the English captives. These adults provided much-needed labor in underpopulated Canada. This was also true of children who had been taken and who could be taught to forget their origins and learn the new language and the new religion. English children were easier to integrate into French society than Native ones. English adults worked as house servants, farmers, and laborers along with French immigrants. They were given a surprising degree of freedom unless they tried to flee captivity, in which case they were severely tortured.

By the end of 1707, almost four years after the Deerfield raid, fifty-two of the one hundred and eleven captives had returned, forty-six as a result of negotiation and ransom. Five had escaped. The forty-seventh, Ebenezer Carter, one of the four Carters who survived the trip to Canada, was brought to Albany, New York, and sold by his Native captors for the sum of twenty-four pounds. He was then ten years old. He was returned to his father, Samuel, living in Norwalk, Connecticut. Ebenezer married in about 1720 and, it was said, had a large family. His two brothers and sister remained captives in Canada. Including these three, thirty-six Deerfield residents remained in the St. Lawrence River Valley: twenty-three were in French communities, and the remaining thirteen lived with the Hurons, the Iroquois of the Mountain, and the Mohawks at Kahnawake. The latter was the largest of the Native villages, with eight to nine hundred residents, located across the St. Lawrence River from Montreal. Mercy Carter, sister of John and Ebenezer, was living at Kahnawake with the Mohawks. Mercy was fourteen years old in 1707. She would marry a Native man in a Catholic church and have several children. Two of her sons in 1751 would visit Carter relatives in Norwalk, but Kahnawake remained her home for the rest of her life. Mercy's cousin Mary Field likewise married a Native and remained in New France. Eunice Williams, daughter of Deerfield minister John Williams, had an almost identical experience as Mercy Carter. Being the daughter of such a prominent captive, her life was well documented.

These Deerfield captives who remained in New France were held by bonds of religion and family. The children were most susceptible to conversion and integration into French society. To help with that process were two orders of the Roman Catholic Church. The most important and also the strictest was the Sulpicians (for the boys). The other was the Congregation of Notre Dame (for the girls). Their mission from King Louis XIV was to go to New France to convert the heathen (which included the Protestant English in his view), and in that they were very successful.

The Congregation de Saint-Sulpice was founded in Paris in 1641 by a French priest, Jean-Jacques Olier, one of a group that was dedicated to training candidates for the priesthood. He established a seminary in Paris when he became pastor of Saint-Sulpice in 1645. In the 1660s the Sulpicians were given large landholdings—*seigneuries*—on Montreal Island in the St. Lawrence River, where they were to conduct their mission of ministering to the Natives and French people living there. They were considered to be more committed in matters of dogma and morals than the Jesuits—a more liberal order. Their seminary building dates from 1661.

When the Deerfield captives came to Montreal, the Sulpicians were headed by a priest, Henri Antoine Meriel de Meulan. He had arrived in 1690 at the age of twenty-nine. He knew the English language, and with a personal fortune he promoted evangelizing efforts. For over twenty years he presided over baptisms, conversions, and marriages of English captives around Montreal. At least thirteen Deerfield captives converted to Roman Catholicism under his guidance. One of these was John Carter, who had changed his name to Jean Chartier.

The Sulpicians had missions in many towns and villages beyond Montreal Island and up the Richelieu River. One leading priest, Father François Vachon de Belmont, explained their belief: "We believe that they [the students] profit by living among us, and not in their own land; that they must be taught our language, that women wear skirts and their men hats and pants; that they must adopt French housing; learn animal husbandry, and how to sow wheat and root vegetables; and that they must be able to read and hear mass and be taught the holy rites."[12] Belmont taught boys to speak, read, and write French, and to sing Latin canticles in church. They learned about Christianity and embraced the Catholic faith. They were successful with most of their students. Jean Chartier would begin a new life, reaping the benefits he was given in material goods in addition to his faith.

Samuel Carter, who had lost most of his family in the Deerfield raid, remained in that town for a year or so searching for word of those who were still alive from the captives who did return. One of them was the Reverend Williams, who told him about those who had perished on the march to Canada and about the four who survived safely and were somewhere in the Montreal area. Knowing of his wife Hannah's death, Samuel married for the third time, to Lois Sention/St. John, in 1706, and moved to New Canaan, Connecticut, not far from Norwalk. His search for his four went on and he was able to secure the release of Ebenezer in 1707. Again thanks to the intervention of Reverend Williams, in 1714 he learned of the death in a drowning accident in the St. Lawrence River of his son, Samuel Jr., twenty-two years old at the time. He tried to repatriate his children John and Mercy "by offering John 500 pounds if he would live permanently in New England and Mercy 100 pounds if she would live in Norwalk with her Kahnawake family for ten years. Neither accepted his offer."[13] Samuel and his wife Lois had one child, a girl they called Lois. Samuel died in Norwalk in September 1728 at the age of about sixty-three.

John Carter, after his conversion to Jean Chartier in 1710 at fourteen years of age, officially became a naturalized citizen of New France. He was thence no longer an Englishman in the Colony of Massachusetts Bay. Under Governor Vaudreuil's regulations he could not return voluntarily or by ransom. He was no longer a prisoner, but a Frenchman. By then he was fluent in French and had been schooled by the Sulpicians for several years. The French were at the zenith of their influence in New France. Their King Louis XIV was truly the Sun King. He had ruled for sixty-seven years and had made his country the dominant power in the world. Only the British would contest this claim, which they did by constant wars against France. The War of Spanish Succession was settled by the Treaty of Utrecht in 1713, with France giving Nova Scotia and Newfoundland to the English. They also had to acknowledge the English claim of sovereignty over the Five Nations of the Iroquois League. The English had lost over four hundred colonists to French and Indian raids on its borders and thirty-six former residents of Deerfield were still in New France. For the rest of the eighteenth century, French influence and power was on the decline.

Jean Chartier
1718 to 1772

Since his capture in 1704, Jean Chartier lived on the lands around Montreal Island in the St. Lawrence River and on the land along the seventy-five-mile-long Richelieu River, which flows north to join the St. Lawrence at the town of Sorel (see map). Some of the villages on Montreal Island were Montreal itself and La Montagne on the south side; and Sault-au-Récollet and Rivière-des-Prairies on the north side. On the south side of the St. Lawrence River across from Montreal were the five different locations of Kahnawake where the Iroquois Nation had their large community, then east to La Prairie, Longueuil, Boucherville, Contrecoeur, and Sorel. On the Richelieu River north to south were St. Antoine, Chambly, St. Jean, and Lake Champlain. This was the greater Montreal region that became Jean's home after 1710 when he was legally naturalized a Canadian, married, and became a significant landowner in several parts of the area. In all of the villages there was a small Native population in addition to a French one. On Montreal Island the Sulpicians owned much of the land as *seigneuries* given to them by the king, and they were committed to turning English captives into good French Catholics and landowners as well. Chartier would benefit from this policy.

On October 29, 1718, at the relatively young age of twenty-three (for a Canadian man), Jean Chartier married Marie Courtemanche, the daughter of Antoine Courtemanche and Marguerite Vaudry. Marguerite's parents, Jacques and Jeanne Renaud, had emigrated from La Rochelle in France. Jean Chartier and his bride, who had been born in 1690 in Montreal, were married in the house of a friend in Pointe-aux-Trembles. It was witnessed by Freedom French Daveny, who herself had been a Deerfield captive in 1704, as was the bridegroom. Freedom had married a Frenchman and remained in New France. She had settled in Montreal and had eleven children, only four of whom lived to adulthood. She kept close ties with the community of English captives.

Soon after their marriage the Chartiers first child, a son they named Joseph, was born on August 21, 1719, in Rivière-des-Prairies where they had settled. Ten more children would follow. The family was doing well in what was expected of them by their church and by their country: to build up the population.

Property was wealth, then as now. The Sulpicians were generous with their gifts of land to those they brought up and educated. By being so, they attracted more to their order as students, if not priests. Montreal Island was large and fertile. If one was clever, money could be made from land sales or from foresting and lumbering. There was good evidence that Jean Chartier prospered greatly.

Following their marriage in 1718, Jean and Marie moved to Rivière-des-Prairies where they received a plot of land from the Sulpicians. Presumably there was a house there or they built one. He acquired more land in Rivières in 1721 and 1722. It is also reported that he and a fellow Deerfield captive, Thomas Hurst, had received land in Sault-au-Récollet from the Sulpicians upon their release from servitude. This gift likely preceded the one in 1718. These two villages were near each other on the northeast point of Montreal Island, several miles distant from Montreal city.

Unlike the English system of common law that gave to the husband all the

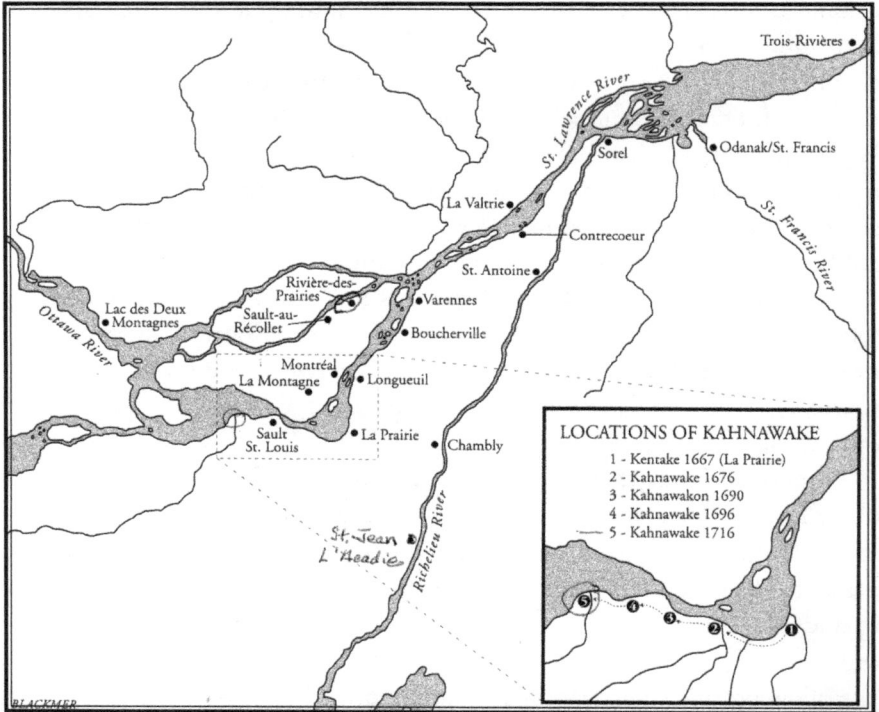

The area pictured above was where John Carter/Jean Chartier grew up and lived from 1704 to his death in 1772. His children and grandchildren also lived in New France, later called Quebec province of Canada.

rights involving the ownership of property, the laws of New France provided that property was "marital community" owned equally by both husband and wife; contracts required the signature of both. But the laws also stated that "the husband is the master of the marital community," so he still had an advantage in case of a disagreement. Divorce was not permitted in that Roman Catholic country, but a separation of goods and property was possible so that a wife could hold goods and property as well as transact business under her own name.

Jean and Marie Chartier remained in Rivière-des-Prairies until 1728. Their first six children were born there: Joseph in 1719, Marie-Renee in 1721, Marie-Angelique in 1723, Jacques in 1725, Jean-Baptiste in 1726, Pierre in 1727. Two of these, Marie-Renée and Pierre, died in infancy. The family moved that year to the village of Contrecoeur on the south bank of the St. Lawrence River about thirty miles downriver (northeast) from Montreal. It was there that Marie-Josephe was born in 1729, and twins Jacques and Pelagie in 1731 and Théodore in 1734.

In the *seigneurie* of Contrecoeur, his new *seigneur* was a comrade-in-arms of Hertel de Rouville, leader of the 1704 Deerfield raid. François-Antoine de Pecaudy de Contrecoeur had worked hard to develop his land and must have given Jean and Marie Chartier favorable terms to leave Montreal Island. The new arrangement worked well for both parties, for in 1732 and 1734 they acquired more land and settled in Contrecoeur's parish of St. Antoine sur Richelieu. This small village, located on the west bank of the river not far from Contrecoeur, became the seat of the Chartier family, their children, and grandchildren from about 1734.

The twenty years from the 1730s to the 1750s were more peaceful in New England and New France as the mother countries were not at war. The frontier between them had moved west from the Connecticut River Valley to the Hudson River-Lake Champlain waterway after the end of the Fourth Anglo-Abenaki War in 1727, and it was there that conflicts were occurring between the Native people, the French, and the English. In 1731 the French completed Fort Frederick at Crown Point, New York, near the head of Lake Champlain, in an attempt to control commerce along the waterway from New York to Canada. Another fort, Carillon, between Lakes Champlain and George at Ticonderoga eight miles to the south, would follow in 1755. The Hertel family of

Chambly oversaw construction at Fort Frederick, and subsequently commanded that post. The English countered this French effort by opening up a new route west from the Connecticut River to Otter Creek in Vermont and then seventy miles down the creek to Lake Champlain at Vergennes, bypassing both French forts. This became a trade route and later a pathway for lumber to a sawmill built in Vergennes in 1783 by John Strong, the earliest English settler on the east bank of the lake. (See Part III, page 105.)

The English also built Fort Dummer in 1724 on the Connecticut River by Brattleboro to prevent attacks by the Natives from the north such as the earlier raids on Deerfield and Northfield. Deerfield itself reflected this westward movement of the frontier by becoming a more normal New England town after 1750—no longer central to trade, diplomacy, and war. New settlers pushed upriver north of Northfield. The New Englanders in Deerfield and elsewhere began to see themselves as native people, and their main concern was no longer the Indians or the French but instead the king and parliament in England, which in 1766 would impose a tax on stamps. They had no say about this, no representative in London, a situation that they called "tyranny."

The years between 1730 to 1750 were a time of economic growth as well. Jean Chartier expanded his land holdings and undertook other ventures, as chronicled in *Captors and Captives*:

> He specialized in developing frontier lands, which he subsequently sold or passed on to his children, then moved on to the next edge of French settlement. He also became involved in fur trading—still an important source of wealth—then lumbering, a new source of wealth launched in part by New England captives who showed the French how to build sawmills. He developed business contacts with Montreal merchants. In 1724 he signed on briefly as a voyageur for Paul Marin de la Malgue, commander of Fort La Baie in what is now Green Bay, Wisconsin. La Malgue was also a fur trader. In 1746 Chartier formed a partnership with Françoise-Louise de Ramezay, the daughter of the one-time governor of Montreal. They built a sawmill at a creek on the Richelieu River still known as *ruisseau* Chartier (Carter Creek).
>
> He continued to make land deals for the rest of his life, and his interest in lumbering led him to look upriver on the Richelieu to the Champlain Valley. In the 1750s his children were starting to marry and settle in the Chambly region. He gave lands at Contrecoeur to his

children in 1751, sold off more, and moved south. In 1754 he bought some land in the *seigneurie* of Longueuil, which extended to the shores of Lake Champlain. This property he put in the name of his sons Joseph and Théodore and his niece, Catherine, the daughter of his sister Mercy who continued to live in Kahnawake with her Native husband. With the beginning of the Seven Years' War in 1755 and the fighting between the English and French on Lake Champlain, Chartier moved north away from the lake to Longueuil, across the river from Montreal, where Marie, his wife, died in 1760.[14]

In his sixties then and nearing the end of his life, he was still dealing with land sales there before returning to the family seat at St. Antoine. He died at home on August 5, 1772, at the age of seventy-six, having spent sixty-two years as a citizen of his adopted country of New France.

During his last years, Jean Chartier had watched his country fight one more war with its traditional enemy, Great Britain. The Seven Years' War, or the French and Indian War as it is called in many American history books, occurred from 1755 to 1763. It could be considered the first world war, as many European nations struggled against each other on land and at sea. In North America it began on Lake George, New York, in September 1755, with British attacks on French and Indian trading routes, while the French hurriedly completed Fort Carillon on the waterway between Lakes George and Champlain at the village of Ticonderoga. The British realized that a much larger force was needed to capture both Fort Carillon and Fort Frederick.

It wasn't until 1758 that Great Britain sent two expeditions across the Atlantic made up of regular army troops—the famed Redcoats—one under General James Abercromby, to attack the two French forts on Lake Champlain from the south, and a second under General Jeffrey Amherst, to attack Fort Louisbourg, the fortified seaport on Cape Breton Island in the Gulf of St. Lawrence. Both generals had difficult tasks, as French forts were well built with centuries of European expertise. Both attacking forts such as in Yorktown and defending them was a science taught French officers at the school of the master, Vauban. At Ticonderoga the French had one of their best generals, Louis Joseph, Marquis de Montcalm de Saint Véran.

Two years earlier, General Montcalm had been appointed commander in chief in New France, subordinate only to Governor Vaudreuil. To assist him in

the important role of surgeon-major of the troops was his friend André Arnoux. The general was the godfather to one of Arnoux's children as well.*
Montcalm had successfully captured Fort Ontario in Oswego in 1757, thereby gaining control of the lake, and also Fort William Henry on Lake George. In 1758 at Ticonderoga, with a force of 3,800 men, he successfully defended the fort by fighting off a much larger British troop of 15,000 men led by General James Abercromby. This failure of the British was due to poor leadership on Abercromby's part and would cause his replacement in the following year by General Jeffrey Amherst. Montcalm's reputation was enhanced, giving the French some hope that they might ultimately triumph. Surgeon-major Arnoux was with Montcalm at Ticonderoga (on July 8, 1758) but was assigned to the Île aux Noix and thus not with his friend in Quebec the following year.

Jeffrey Amherst had come from an outstanding victory in 1758 with the capture of the French fortress of Louisbourg. This victory meant that the French could supply their colony only by the St. Lawrence River to Quebec, and it gave the British navy a nearby base to attack French supply vessels, noticeably weakening the future of New France.

In 1759 the pincers began closing on the French colony. The British sent a new expedition under General James Wolfe to go up the St. Lawrence River to attack and capture Quebec City, the capital. Simultaneously on Lake Champlain, General Jeffrey Amherst attacked a weakened French force, captured Fort Frederick and Fort Carillon, and, bypassing Montreal, proceeded down the St. Lawrence River toward Quebec to join up with the main British force under General Wolfe. Montcalm, earlier in the year, had moved to Quebec to defend the capital city and prepare for a major battle. Both men knew that should Great Britain win, France would lose their colony and it would become another part of the fast-growing British empire.

In September 1759, although General Amherst's group had not yet reached Quebec, General Wolfe surprised General Montcalm by taking five thousand men up the St. Lawrence at night to the west of the city where they went ashore and climbed up the cliffs to the high ground, thereby sealing off any retreat possible for Montcalm. With dawn an open battle began on the Plains

---

*   André Arnoux was born in St. Paul de Vence, an old medieval town on the French Riviera. The son of Alexandré Arnoux, also a surgeon-major, André had chosen to practice his profession in the king's navy, taking part, it is said, in twelve battles at sea before being sent to New France in 1751 to serve in Montreal. Due to the unexpected death of the previous surgeon-major of the troops, André was appointed to succeed him in 1755.

British navy vessels attacking a French fortress such as Fort Louisbourg in 1758.

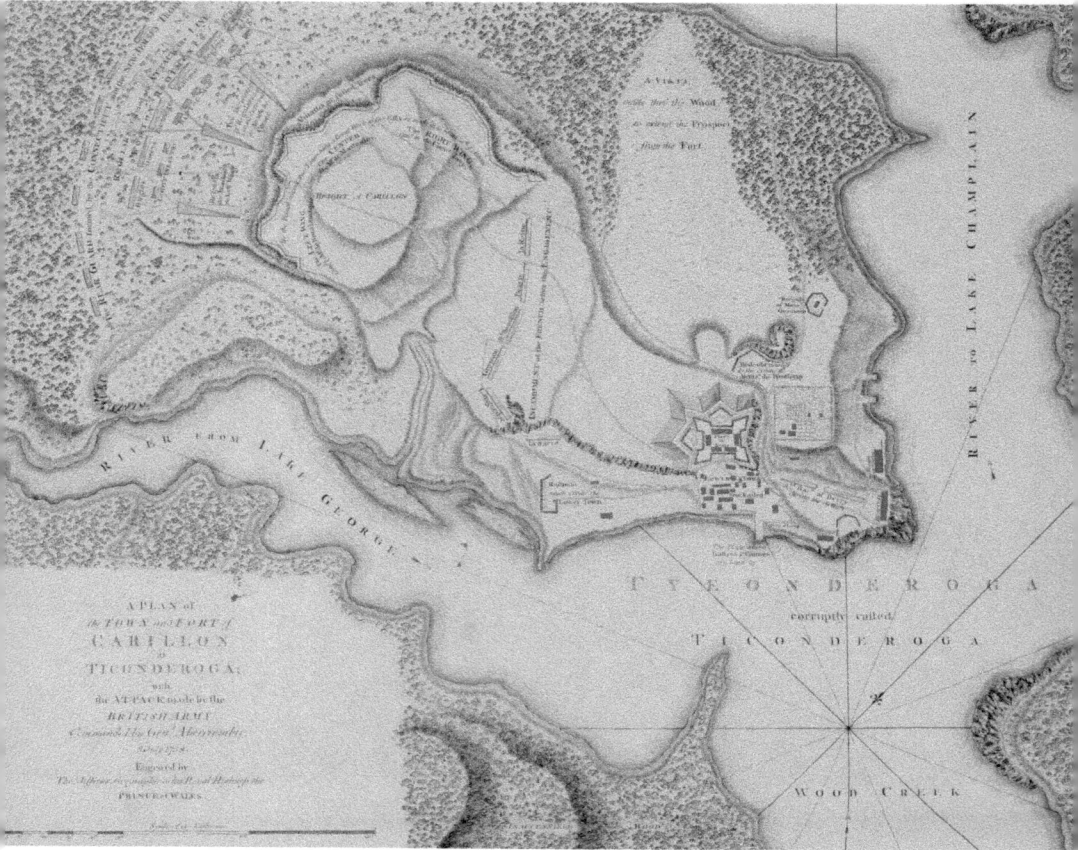

General Montcalm defeated the British attempt to capture Fort Carillon at Ticonderoga in 1758. It was his greatest triumph in the war.

of Abraham, which the Redcoats won. With no French retreat possible they surrendered. Both Wolfe and Montcalm died that day from wounds inflicted in the battle.

Although the formal peace treaty was not signed until four years later, France lost its colony in the North American continent that day. In 1760, General Amherst captured a small remaining French group in Montreal and took charge of the city. All resistance had ended.

General Montcalm's friend surgeon-major André Arnoux remained in the outskirts of Quebec to tend the wounds of all wounded in the battle, English and French alike, at the Hospital General. That summer Arnoux went to Montreal, where on August 20, 1760, he died of an inflammation of the lungs, probably a casualty of war as well. Along with Montcalm, Arnoux was a leader in the war and was well known in the French community of the Montreal area. During his years in New France from 1751 to 1760 it is very likely that he had become acquainted with Jean Chartier, the wealthy landowner on the Richelieu River. And it is certainly possible that Chartier was acquainted with General Montcalm as well.

In the Treaty of Paris, signed in 1763, France agreed to surrender all the remaining parts of their colony New France to the British. Fifty years earlier in 1713 in the Treat of Utrecht they had turned over Acadia, which the British named Nova Scotia, Newfoundland, and the Hudson Bay territory. Now all the rest of Canada and all claims of land east of the Mississippi River, including the Ohio Valley, were also conceded. New France had been overwhelmed by superior numbers of soldiers, sailors, warships, and cannon. Never before had any nation spent so much money to win a war on a transoceanic scale. The British would look to recover some of these funds by assessing higher taxes on their colony in America.

Joseph Chartier in Canada
1719–1776

For the French-speaking, mostly Catholic people of Quebec province in Canada, 1763 was a milestone year. The country that they had grown up believing was their enemy was now their master, and anti-Catholic as well. Most of the Native tribes that had been pro-French—with the exception of the Iroquois Nation—had to change their affiliation. Many of them moved westward to the upper Great Lakes. In the Richelieu River Valley, Jean Chartier was sixty-eight that year. His oldest son, Joseph, who would become head of the family, was forty-four. They knew that their lives would change. Their loyalties were to France, and Great Britain was still the enemy.

Joseph Chartier had been born on August 21, 1719, in Rivière-des-Prairies while his mother and father were living there. On June 7, 1751, he married Marie Ursule Hubert, daughter of Pierre Paul Hubert and Suzanne La Porte, who was ten years younger than her husband. The Hubert family was living in Contrecoeur, and the couple must have become acquainted as the Chartier family were living there as well in the 1730s. After their marriage the couple lived at the Chartier homestead in St. Antoine, and it was there that seven children were born, five sons and two daughters, the youngest daughter being Marie Cecile Chartier born August 1, 1770. All but the last two were born before the French defeat in 1763.

Although the Richelieu River Valley was the path of General Amherst's attack on Montreal in 1760, towns such as Contrecoeur and St. Antoine were too small to have suffered much. Still, they had experienced the presence of British Redcoats in both 1759 and 1760. The sons of the Chartiers were young children at that time, but absorbed the resentment felt in their families about their British masters. The British army would not be a presence in their lives again until 1775 when sons Pierre and Jean were nineteen and seventeen years old.

General Wolfe defeated General Montcalm on the Plains of Abraham in Quebec in 1759, ending French control of New France.

PART II

The French Contribution to the War of Independence

1775–1783

The "Shot Heard Round the World"

When the famous shot was fired on April 19, 1775, by the patriot farmers at the Redcoats in Concord, Massachusetts, the sound reverberated all the way to the Richelieu Valley. Pierre and Jean Chartier, sons of Joseph, heard it and applauded those brave farmers who had dared fire at and kill British soldiers. Being young and adventuresome, they wanted to join the cause. Only a month later, in May, word reached the valley that the Green Mountain Boys of Vermont under their leaders Ethan Allen and Benedict Arnold had attacked and overrun the British garrisons at Fort Ticonderoga and Fort Frederick on Lake Champlain. A windfall of cannons and military stores would be taken overland to the patriots outside of Boston, who desperately needed them.

Then, in the fall of 1775, the Chartier sons saw their chance. General George Washington, by then having been appointed commander in chief by the Second Continental Congress, had high hopes of an invasion of Canada led by General Richard Montgomery and Colonel Benedict Arnold. The goal was to capture Quebec City and thus prevent the British from attacking the United States from the north. Montgomery was to proceed north up the Hudson-Champlain-Richelieu-St. Lawrence route, considered the easier way, and Arnold from Massachusetts through Maine to Canada and Quebec. They would rendezvous in mid-December outside the walled city, and Washington was confident that they would prevail.

It was not to be. Arnold's force was slowed by heavy rains, swollen streams, and fierce rapids as they passed through the Maine forests. The troops had not been properly provided for. Many starved and some deserted. When they did finally reach Quebec they were in disarray and had to wait for Montgomery. The general, the higher ranking of the two, had easier terrain to cover and the better weather, but he ran into much more British resistance, which took more time. There were British forces in the Richelieu Valley and in Montreal. Although the French population was friendly to him, he had battles to win at St. Jean, Chambly, and Montreal before getting eastward to Quebec. Arriving at the very end of December, the combined force suffered a shattering defeat. General Montgomery died in battle on December 31, 1775. Colonel Arnold received a musket ball in the leg, giving him a permanent limp. Worst of all, the strategic plan failed and the inexperienced troops lost their nerve and fled in panic. The British held Quebec with minor casualties, and what remained of the two expeditions retreated back to where they had started—a severe setback for Washington. The Richelieu Valley towns, along with Montreal, were in the hands of Montgomery's army for a short time, until they retreated back to Albany in the early spring of 1776, leaving them again in British control. The valley was said to be badly damaged in the fighting, but from the colonists' point of view it was not all bad, as 250 residents of the area enlisted in the Second Canadian Regiment. Two of those men were young Pierre and Jean Chartier.

Moses Hazen and the Canadian Regiment

The history of the new Canadian regiment began in 1775 before the attempt to capture Quebec by General Montgomery and Colonel Arnold. Montgomery, who had earlier served as a soldier in the British army during the capture of Louisbourg, Ticonderoga, and Montreal in 1758 and 1759, returned to New York in 1772 to marry a daughter of Robert L. Livingston, wealthy Hudson River landowner. In 1775, by then a Brigadier General, he was asked to recruit an army to attack and capture Quebec City in support of the American Revolution in tandem with Arnold. Assisting him was Colonel James Livingston, of his wife's family, who had raised and commanded a troop of American militia from New York together with Canadians from the greater Montreal area who were opposed to British rule, one of whom was Théodore Chartier, the youngest son of Jean and Marie Chartier and the uncle of Pierre and Jean. Livingston's regiment of about three hundred men—two hundred and fifty Canadians and fifty Americans—fought a battle at St. Jean and at Chambly on the way north prior to Montgomery's capture of Montreal. While fighting at St. Jean in November that year, the regiment destroyed the home and growing estate of a man who had served the British during the Seven Years' War as a lieutenant, was receiving a British pension, but was at birth and at heart an American. His name was Moses Hazen. At the time of the battle of St. Jean, Hazen was held by the British in Montreal for spying for the Americans, but was released when Montgomery captured the city to join the cause and the attack on Quebec.

Following the failure at Quebec and the death of Montgomery, Hazen went to Philadelphia to report to the Congress and convinced them to officially authorize the Second Canadian Regiment, which they did on January 20, 1776. Moses Hazen was named its colonel and commanding officer. It soon became known as "Hazen's Regiment" or "Congress's Own." (Most militias in the War of Independence were raised by states of the Union and were not federal.) Its strength varied between 250 men in the beginning, to a high of 720 men in 1778. At the start most men were from Canada, whereas later men from Pennsylvania joined this unit. At Montreal in February 1776 Colonel Hazen began to recruit in the nearby communities to add to those who had survived at Quebec from Livingston's nucleus. From then until April in the St. Lawrence and Richelieu River Valleys he was able to bring the regiment up to about 250 men. It was in this interval that the Chartier brothers joined Hazen's Regiment.

A few words about Colonel Moses Hazen himself: Born in Haverhill, Massachusetts, in 1733, the son of a merchant of the same name, he enlisted in the British army during its successful attacks against the French, culminating in its capture of Quebec in 1759. Following this (he was twenty-two years old) he purchased a lieutenant's commission in a British regiment in 1761 but soon returned in 1763 at the war's end.

Hazen then decided to settle in Montreal where he had fought much earlier, and he became an entrepreneur. By then he must have been fluent in French, the language spoken throughout Quebec, and his sympathies must have turned against the British and for the French Canadians and their allies, the American colonists. With another man he developed a lumbering business on Lake Champlain and settled on a part of two *seigneuries* he purchased on the east bank of the Richelieu River at St. Jean where he had farms. In 1770 he was formally designated a *seigneur* of Bleury-Sud, and although much younger, he may have known the senior Jean Chartier of St. Antoine, thirty miles or so down the river from St. Jean, or some of his sons.

With the advent of the War of Independence in 1775 and because Hazen's lands lay along the American invasion route, he was arrested first by the Americans for being a British lieutenant and possible spy, and then by the British who confined him in Montreal. Following the capture of the city by Montgomery, Hazen was released by his captors and joined Montgomery on the road to Quebec. The one-time British lieutenant had proven his new loyalty to the American cause. Although his home at St. Jean was in ruin as was much of the Richelieu River Valley, Hazen returned to Montreal to recruit for the new regiment. He was briefly the commander at Montreal in the spring of 1776 until the regiment was ordered south in April.

The Evacuation from Canada

After the failure to invade and occupy Canada in 1775 and 1776, General Washington wanted as many troops as possible to return to the New York City area, where he anticipated the main British army under General Howe would attack next. He also wanted one of his best generals, Benedict Arnold, where he could be more effective in the invasion to come. Thus in the spring of 1776 Hazen's Canadian Regiment left the Richelieu Valley with about 250 men, mostly French Canadians, for Fort Ticonderoga, thence to Albany on the Hudson River and finally to Fishkill, New York, where the Continental army had established a major camp. The Congress had also established refugee camps there and at Albany with rations for families who had departed Canada along with Hazen's Regiment. The regiment wintered at Fishkill in 1776–1777 and on January 8 was assigned to the main Continental army.

Hazen's Regiment, 1777-1781

Two of the three most important battles of the war in which the regiment played a role were the Battles of Brandywine and Germantown. During these the regiment was under the overall command of Division General John Sullivan. With new recruits from Pennsylvania, it was about seven hundred men strong, its all-time high. On September 11 at Brandywine Creek the regiment was credited with first spotting British troops making a flanking maneuver to cross the creek. However, General Washington at first did not believe their report and delayed reacting to it, thus permitting the army of British General Howe to achieve a major victory on its way to occupy the capital city of Philadelphia. Hazen's Regiment lost four officers and seventy-three men in the battle.

Later in the fall of that year, on October 4, when the British were encamped at Germantown, Pennsylvania, northwest of Philadelphia, Washington planned a bold attack at dawn after a seventeen-mile march to surprise Howe. The attack was led by General Sullivan's force including Hazen's men. Unfortunately the element of surprise was lost and the fog was so thick at dawn that it was impossible to tell who was the enemy. The effort failed and the American army lost 150 killed, 520 wounded, and 400 captured, three times more than the British. Three officers and nineteen men of Hazen's Regiment were lost as well.

This second major defeat for General Washington and the dreadful winter at Valley Forge that followed ended the year at a low ebb. There was only one bright spot for the new country, which would be like the rising sun. While Washington was losing at Germantown, his Generals Horatio Gates and Benedict Arnold had defeated British General John Burgoyne at Saratoga, New York. French foreign minister Count de Vergennes was very impressed with both the Saratoga victory and the American willingness to launch an attack in Germantown, even though it failed. "The American would fight," he told his new king, Louis XVI. "We will have to help them."

Hazen's Regiment did not fight again until at Yorktown in 1781, but it was not idle. In 1778 it was sent to Albany for a planned invasion of Canada, which was called off. It was then ordered to West Point, and finally to White Plains to watch over British-held New York. Its manpower declined and Washington considered disbanding it because it had too many officers—thirty-three—for its diminishing number of men, by years end only 162, and those were "unfit for duty for want of shoes."[15] In 1779, Hazen, always eager to invade Canada to get his lands back from the British occupation, suggested building a military road across northeastern Vermont following the path of an old Cohassiac Indian trail from Lower Coös in lower New Hampshire to St. Jean, his *seigneurie*. The road cut across what is today the Northeast Kingdom of Vermont. The road was actually built by the regiment to the Canadian border. Known as the Bayley-Hazen Military Road, it was within forty miles of St. Jean on June 22, 1779, when the regiment was recalled the New York area to help contain British raids on the northern towns of Pound Ridge and Bedford. Fifty-four miles of road had been built, ending at Hazen's notch.

The year 1780 was again one of travel for the regiment. A "commando" raid on Staten Island in New York in January was planned and aborted. Summer was spent at King's Point, and on October 2, one hundred of Hazen's soldiers were detailed to be present at the hanging of Lieutenant John André, British soldier and captured spy, at Tappan, New York. The year 1781 started out the same way, with a raid on Morrisania in the Bronx, the burning of British barracks there, and the taking of prisoners and ammunitions. Then the regiment was sent to Mohawk Valley in Albany to guard against a British attack—that never came—before returning to West Point. Finally, on June 29, Hazen was promoted to brevet brigadier general, the rank he would hold when, on August 10, word came that the "Congress's Own" was going south with the main army. No destination was given, only to report to Fishkill for orders.[16]

The Role of France in the War of Independence, 1774–1780

The Treaty of Paris was signed in 1763, ending the conflict between Great Britain and France and their allies, which had been fought on land and at sea throughout much of the world since 1756. It was known as the Seven Years' War, except in America where it was called the French and Indian War. It "was the making of William Pitt, the Elder, prime minister of King George III and perhaps of the First British Empire."[17] The French were driven out of India, lost their Caribbean colony of Guadeloupe, and were defeated in Canada at Louisbourg, Quebec, and Montreal, losing New France completely, as has been noted. British naval historian Tom Pocock called the Seven Years' War "the very first world war because the combatants, Britain allied with Prussia and Portugal against France, Austria, and latterly, Spain, campaigned in both hemispheres and on every continent and ocean."[18] At its end, the entire eastern seaboard of North America was British, which had repercussions in the War of Independence soon to follow. Without the French, the American colonists became less dependent on the British, and the British were free to prohibit American migration west of the Alleghany Mountains, which angered the expansionist-minded settlers.

For France, the Treaty of Paris was an embarrassing defeat. Crushed militarily on land and at sea, stripped of colonies by the treaty, it lost its position as a leading European nation to become a second-rate power. The goal of its foreign policy became revenge against its historical enemy. France's King Louis XV was nearing the end of his long reign. It was said that his mistress, Madame de Pompadour, had managed the French foreign policy during the Seven Years' War, but she died in 1764 and was succeeded by Madame du Barry. Her favorite, François de Choiseul, continued to control foreign affairs until 1770. In 1774, Louis XV died and was succeeded by Louis XVI, not yet twenty years old, who appointed an experienced diplomat as minister for foreign affairs: Charles Gravier, Comte de Vergennes. He would become a staunch friend of the new country on the North American continent.

Vergennes, a clever and subtle statesman, had observed during the Seven Years' War that if France lost Canada, "England will soon repent of having removed the only check that could keep her colonies in awe. They stand no longer in need of her protection. She will call on them to contribute toward supporting the burdens they have helped to bring on her, and they will answer by striking off all dependence."[19] It was a very farsighted prediction of events in 1775–76. He was wise enough to be content with humbling England, while avoiding the impression that France was seeking her destruction.

In 1775, discussions began in France about ways to help the American colonists with arms and money. Included in them was the Spanish foreign minister, as Spain could benefit as well as France. Reasons to do so included weakening the power of England and increasing that of France; the loss of English trade and the increase of French trade; and the recovery of fisheries off Newfoundland and in the Gulf of St. Lawrence. "We do not speak of Canada," the memoir concluded.[20] That was for the colonists to decide.

On May 12, 1776 (two months before July 4, 1776—Independence Day), France agreed to pursue a policy of secret assistance to the colonists in America. Louis XVI directed that one million livres' worth of munitions be delivered from royal arsenals in the islands of Martinique and Haiti to American agents and reshipped to the colonies. After signing the Declaration of Independence, the Continental Congress sent an official mission to France headed by Benjamin Franklin, the best-known American in the world at the time. He notified Vergennes that the mission was empowered by the Congress to propose and negotiate a treaty of commerce between their two countries. Perhaps more than any other American, Franklin would promote the welfare of the new country and ensure its support by the French nation; but that would not come right away.

In 1777, three men were sent to the United States because of Franklin's efforts. The first was a nineteen-year-old French aristocrat with a very long name: Marie Joseph Paul Yves Roch Gilbert du Montier, Marquis de Lafayette. This young nobleman was at first received coldly by Congress, but later was commissioned a major general without command—as a volunteer without pay—and assigned to Washington. His help in bringing French support would be notable in the future. The second was a German nobleman, Baron Friedrich Wilhelm von Steuben, who had served on the general staff of Frederick the Great. His help in training American soldiers would make an important contribution to the effort. The third was a French officer who would later play a significant role in the Battle of Yorktown. Louis Le Bègue Duportail was by training an engineer. He had spent his early years studying the methods of conducting a siege developed by French Marshal Sébastien Le Prestre de Vauban under Louis XIV. This military strategy was unknown to Americans but was successfully used in Europe and would be at Yorktown. Duportail became the chief engineer for George Washington and was made a Brigadier General in 1777. For a time he was captured by the British in South Carolina but was released in a prisoner exchange.

During the dark times that year when the British under General Howe were occupying Philadelphia, after having defeated Washington the year before in Long Island and New York, Franklin in France waited for some good news to come from home. It was late on December 4 when he received word that General Burgoyne and his whole army were prisoners of war. The Battle at Saratoga in October had resulted in the first victory over British armies. Seizing the moment, Franklin approached Vergennes and asked for recognition; on December 17, 1777, Franklin was notified that His Majesty Louis XVI was ready to acknowledge the independence of the United States and enter into a treaty of amity and commerce.

On February 6, 1778, the treaty was signed by Vergennes for the French nation and by Franklin, Lee, and Deane for the United States of America. In addition to recognizing its independence, other provisions embodied most-favored-nation trading privileges. An important second treaty provided that in the event of war between France and Great Britain as a consequence of the first treaty, the United States and France would fight the war together and neither would make peace with the enemy without the formal consent of the other. Also, they would not lay down their arms until the independence of the United States was assured by a treaty ending the war. This second treaty would be of key importance in the events that followed. On the same day the agreement was signed Great Britain declared war on France.

The first French effort to help its new ally after the treaties were signed was a complete failure. In the spring of 1778 a fleet of warships under the command of Count d'Estaing sailed from the Mediterranean. After an incredibly slow crossing of three months, he missed a chance to catch the British fleet in Chesapeake Bay. By the time he arrived there he was low on water with sick men on every ship. After sailing north toward New York he was advised correctly by local pilots that the water depth at Sandy Hook was insufficient for his fleet to cross the bar and enter the Upper Bay. Upon a recommendation from Congress, the fleet sailed to Newport, Rhode Island, with the intention of capturing a three-thousand-man British garrison there, but failed in that endeavor due to poor communication with American General John Sullivan and an unfortunate storm that badly damaged the French fleet. D'Estaing was forced to sail to Boston for repairs, following which he sailed south to South Carolina and Georgia to help the Americans defend against British attacks on Charleston and Savannah in 1779. This was also a failure due to "bickering over just about everything."[21] D'Estaing himself was wounded, and the American and French suffered eight hundred casualties to about sixty for the British. With his men dying of scurvy and fever and the hurricane season approaching, the fleet sailed for France, leaving the Americans bitter about help from any French fleet in the future. Clearly what was needed from their ally was a large ground force supported by naval ships, and in 1779 that was what they promoted and lobbied for.

The French were not surprised by what they considered the poor quality of the American militiamen, and they were skeptical about the leadership of American officers. Rumors had come back to France that training and discipline were inadequate and that American soldiers would not stand and fight when opposed by a staunch and experienced foe. Some may have regretted that an alliance with the new country was ever agreed to. However, due to efforts by Benjamin Franklin in Paris and by Lafayette, who was sent back to France in 1779 to consult with Vergennes and King Louis XVI, a decision was made to send an expeditionary force of ten to twelve thousand veteran troops led by Comte de Rochambeau, and six million livres, protected by seven ships of the line. They would leave by March 1780 and arrive in Rhode Island by June, it was hoped. Their orders were to join the American army to recapture New York City from the British. General Rochambeau was to place himself under the command of General Washington.

Preparations for the Arrival of the French Army

When Washington heard the news of the expeditionary force in April from Lafayette upon his return from Paris, he was, of course, delighted, immediately seeing the hope of a victory over the British in their principal stronghold in America. At the same time, he was embarrassed at the small size and poor condition of his own army that the French would find when they arrived. Writing to the state governors he said, "Were they to arrive today, they would find we have but a handful of men in the field and doubt we had any serious intentions to prosecute measures with vigor."[22] He was fearful that the French fleet might just sail away. American ranks in February 1780 were over 14,000 men short of what was needed, and new recruits by July 4 that year amounted to only thirty men. Washington was forced to again appeal to state governors, the only source of reinforcements. His own ability was being questioned in Congress, and Generals Horatio Gates and Charles Lee were scheming to undercut and replace him.

The French alliance called for a new approach to strategy and different tactics. Although the British fleet was larger than the French one, both nations had to keep a part of their fleets at home to defend against attack by the other, and Spain had a fleet, allied with France but not under its control. Coordination of fleets by both sides was almost impossible, as messages took weeks to arrive overseas from both London and Paris. Both countries depended on spies to a great extent. Thanks to them, Great Britain knew of the Franco-American treaty before it was signed in Paris. In 1780 and 1781, French Admiral de Grasse (who had succeeded d'Estaing) and Generals Rochambeau and Washington all had difficulty coordinating strategy, as did British Generals Clinton and Cornwallis and Admirals Arbuthnot and Graves. The Admiralty in London often had no idea where their fleets were in the Western Hemisphere, which was a fatal disadvantage to the British at the end. Furthermore, none of the French except Lafayette spoke English or could understand tactical orders from Americans on the field of battle. This would pose problems in planning the attack on Yorktown later on. Washington informed Rochambeau that he would communicate with him through Lafayette, "a friend from whom I conceal nothing—I entreat you to receive whatever he should tell you as coming from me."[23] Washington did not know that in Paris Lafayette had put himself forward for supreme leader of the expeditionary force. He was twenty-three years old at the time. He was rejected by Count Vergennes, and most of the French commanders paid little attention to the "young lad." Rochambeau replied to Washington: "I beg of your Excellency to continue to give me your orders by the same direct means that you have done until now."[24]

The fact that the French fleet could land in Newport, Rhode Island, at all was due to a blunder on the part of the British Admiral Arbuthnot, who would not cooperate with General Clinton, his superior. Clinton had known that Rochambeau's army was bound for Newport from American General Benedict Arnold, who was betraying his country. Clinton, with his large garrison in New York, wanted to occupy Newport before the French arrived but was frustrated because Arbuthnot refused to believe the intelligence and preferred to wait for reinforcements. Clinton thus prepared to attack the French when they were in the process of landing, but again Arbuthnot advised against it. Neither knew when the French would arrive until their frigates were sighted off Virginia on July 5, only to quickly disappear again. A week later British Admiral Graves's squadron arrived from England with seven hundred sick seamen not ready for duty. Again Clinton argued for attack, but Arbuthnot warned that French and American artillery now in Newport would be too much for his ships. No attack was made, and the army of Rochambeau was safely ashore. The failure of the British to attack at Newport was a calamity in the long run. Because of the feud between Clinton and Arbuthnot, Rochambeau's army with veteran units remained unharmed and within an easy sail of New York. Their presence was a constant threat to Clinton. During the summer of 1780 the British lost the initiative and never regained it. Washington was encouraged to believe that a joint French-American attack on New York would be successful and end the war.

The Expeditionary Force

The French force that disembarked in Newport after July 11, 1780, was under the command of Jean-Baptiste-Donatien de Vimeur, Comte de Rochambeau. Born in 1725, the son of the governor of Vendôme on the Loire, he was first headed for a career in the church, but with the early death of his older brother in 1742 he chose to become a cornet in the cavalry regiment of Saint-Simon. This was the beginning of a lifelong military career during which he fought in many battles throughout Europe. He was promoted to captain in 1743; to colonel of the regiment in 1747; was wounded in battle but recovered; in 1755 was made governor of Vendôme succeeding his father; in 1761 was named marechal de camp; and finally in 1780, at the age of fifty-five, was chosen by foreign minister Vergennes to lead the expedition with the rank of Lieutenant General. He was known to be a cautious military strategist, spoke no English, and surprisingly agreed to serve under George Washington. He had his own opinions about strategy but was diplomatic in his relationship with Washington.

The army that Rochambeau led consisted of about six thousand fighting men grouped in six regiments of differing size and experience. Four of these were chosen by him to play leading roles in the final battle at Yorktown. They were the Bourbonnais, the Saintonge, the Soissonnais, and the Royal Deux-Ponts regiments, the latter being of German origin.

Rochambeau was assisted by Antoine Charles du Houx, Baron de Vioménil (born 1728), his second in command; his younger brother the Comte de Vioménil (born 1734), who commanded the French artillery; Chevalier de Chastellux (born 1734), his third in command; Guillaume, Comte de Deux-Ponts (born 1754), a Bavarian who led his regiment with heavy losses at Yorktown; Chevalier Anne-César de la Luzerne (born 1741), who oversaw purchases for the French army and was a go-between for Washington and Rochambeau; Marquis de Saint-Simon (born 1760), who led three thousand men; Louis Le Bègue Duportail, Brigadier General and Commander of the Corps of Engineers at Yorktown; and finally Marquis de Lafayette (born 1757), who served under General Washington but ranked with the above officers with no military experience at all. He did, however, have good command of the English language. Almost all the French officers of high rank, captains and above, were of the French nobility who had chosen a military career for life and had gained great experience in the many military battles in Europe in the eighteenth century.

The French convoy that carried the expedition consisted of forty-six ships carrying upwards of twelve thousand people and was under the command of French Admiral Chevalier de Ternay. Most of the vessels were transports carrying the army and the large supporting personnel. There were only seven ships of the line and five smaller frigates to protect this huge fleet. Thus the southern route was chosen to avoid the British navy, which could have destroyed the expedition completely. The fleet sailed from Brest on May 2 via the Azores to the Caribbean and then northwest to Newport, a voyage of more than two months. A few brief encounters were made with small British squadrons, which reported home that the French were on the way. This prompted the Admiralty to send reinforcements under Admiral Graves to Newport, who failed to arrive until after the French had safely landed. Admirals Graves and Arbuthnot could have blockaded the French in Newport but did so for only a short time.

When Rochambeau and his troop of six thousand men arrived they were in terrible condition after such a long voyage on ships in cramped quarters. The general reported that 2,600 were sick, two-thirds of them suffering from scurvy, and hospital facilities were set up in Newport. One baron wrote that he shared a space with nineteen others. It was fifteen feet long, twelve feet wide, and four and a half feet high. "Not too comfortable [due to] exhalations and other bad odors produced by the passengers," he said.[25] The Deux-Ponts regiment lost nine men during the trip with 450 sick upon arrival. Clearly, Rochambeau was in no hurry to move his army overland. Besides their health, they had no arms, no gunpowder, no uniforms. Admiral Ternay told Washington that a "second division" of ships was on the way—which was not the case—and until they arrived nothing could be done to advance the cause.

Washington's army was in terrible shape as well. Lafayette, who was sent to Newport to greet General Rochambeau on July 24, told him that the American forces amounted to seven thousand men and that Washington intended a siege New York City. The fact was that he did not have enough horses and wagons to join the French in an operation anywhere any time soon. Rochambeau had expected his ally to have a much larger force and was convinced that until more support came from France, he could not move. He sent his son back to France to request another fleet, but it would be early 1781 before that could occur. In the meantime the American officer corps deteriorated and the militias began to return home when their time of service was up. Furthermore, Rochambeau refused to attack New York City without naval supremacy, which he did not have and would not have until another fleet with ships to fight the British ships of the line was sent to North American waters. It seemed like a deadlock had been created, and the war would go on as the hoped-for second division was caught in the British blockage of Brest in France.

Planning Ahead

Meanwhile Washington and Rochambeau were determined to meet and to plan a grand strategy for 1781 that might inflict such damage on the British occupation force under Sir Henry Clinton that they would withdraw and sign a treaty of peace. They planned to meet for the first time in Hartford, Connecticut, on September 20, 1780, a convenient place midway between Newport, Rhode Island, and the Hudson Valley where Washington was located with his army. With the American general were Alexander Hamilton, his secretary and personal aide in charge of planning; Major General Henry Knox, chief of artillery; and Lafayette, who helped with translating. Washington's French was weak, and Rochambeau spoke no English at all. On the French side was his second in command, Baron de Vioménil.

Hamilton had prepared three separate strategies to be presented to the French general. Each depended on when and where the fleet blockaded at Brest would arrive. Rochambeau showed little interest in any of these, only agreeing to attack New York City and only if the French navy controlled the entrance to the harbor.

On a personal level, however, the meeting was friendly. Washington was admired by the French officers. One of these, Comte Mathieu Dumas, said, "His dignified address, his simplicity of manners, and mild gravity surpassed our expectation and won every heart."[26] This positive response by the French somewhat overcame their skepticism of the amateurism of the Americans as fighters. Rochambeau had no illusions about Washington. His orders were "in all cases to be under the orders of General Washington," but a secret instruction (not seen by Washington) added that he was to keep the French troops together, and not to disperse them under any circumstances.[27] He had doubts about the general's judgment in tactical matters. At the end of the conference, Washington said he hoped to have fifteen thousand troops by spring in 1781, and Rochambeau told him that Louis XVI had promised the "second division" to add to their army and that he would send his son to Versailles to request this support.

Washington was disappointed at the end of the Hartford conference. Although it had been a "social success," one more year had gone by without any damage to the British. Victory at Saratoga had occurred three years ago by then, and there had been no others. The French had agreed to join the cause but had not yet been successful in any battle on land or at sea against the British. The winter of 1780–81 would have to be endured by his army—what was left of it—and plans made for the next campaign. Washington knew that much depended on whether the promised "second division"—a French fleet of warships strong enough to tackle the British navy—would arrive to support him and his ally, General Rochambeau, who was waiting in Newport.

Waiting in Newport, Rhode Island

The French army would wait in Newport from July 1780 to June 1781, almost one year. The officers had taken over some of the elegant houses there for the duration of their stay. They did experience the edge of a typical Atlantic hurricane in the autumn of 1780, which drove ships aground, dismasted some others, and blew away many tents that housed the soldiers. For the officers there were dinner parties held and good times had by all. The Bavarian officer, Baron von Closen, aide to Rochambeau, found Rhode Island women "unusual in their modesty and sweetness of demeanor, noting that they had very fine features, white and clear complexions, small hands and feet, but their teeth are not very wonderful; a fault he attributed to drinking great quantities of tea... Fortunately, they all like dancing, and engage in it unpretentiously, as in their manner in general."[28] The Comte de Clermont-Crèvecoeur, another aide of the general, said, "Americans are tall and well built, but thin, which made most of them look as though they have grown while convalescing from an illness."[29] Clermont-Crèvecoeur was twenty-eight years old at the time and had been away from France for six months.

Some officers chose to leave Newport and travel in the United States during the hiatus. One of these, Chevalier de Chastellux, third in command, left Newport in early November to travel to the interior of the country. He wrote a book about his travels in America.[*]

Generally the French and Americans got on well together while living in and around Newport. The exception was with Quakers, of whom there were many in the area. Being Roman Catholic for the most part, the French could not understand their silent religious services, found them grave in dress and manner, and inclined to talk little. Clermont-Crèvecoeur noted, "Their wedding feasts are terribly dreary, since nobody speaks. You may imagine how much fun that would be!"[30]

During the winter of 1780–81, Washington became increasingly pessimistic that a second French fleet would ever set sail. In January, Lafayette had written, "With a naval inferiority it is impossible to make war in America. It is that which prevents us from attacking any point that might be carried with two or three thousand men. It is that which reduces us to defensive operations, as dangerous as they are humiliating."[31] The letter was delivered to the Comte de Vergennes, but no response came. Had the French king given up? Was he fearful of losing a fleet in battle with the British and weakening the French de-

---

[*]   *Travels in North America in Years 1780, 1781, 1782* by François-Jean de Beauvoir, Chevalier de Chastellux.

fenses against an invasion? At this point, when Rochambeau's son and Lafayette had failed, Benjamin Franklin wrote a letter that persuaded Louis XVI and his minister to act. Franklin said that if the English were to recover their former colonies, an opportunity like the present one might never recur, while possession of the vast territory and resources of America would give the English ever-expanding commerce and a supply of seamen and soldiers that would make them "the terror of Europe."

Although the news did not reach Washington until a French frigate docked in Boston on May 8, 1781, it was news he desperately wanted to hear. On March 22 a French fleet under the command of Admiral François Joseph Paul, Comte de Grasse, had departed Brest for the West Indies. In addition to this good news, the son of Rochambeau on the frigate arriving in Boston had with him six million livres to supply the needs of the American army.

However, General Rochambeau received certain news from Vergennes that he did not share with Washington. He knew the main fleet was sailing to the West Indies, but did not reveal how long it would stay there; nor did he reveal that de Grasse had orders to sail north in July or August. Rochambeau knew that Washington wanted to attack New York City, and both men knew that a French squadron would have difficulty crossing the bar at Sandy Hook. Rochambeau would communicate directly with de Grasse that the Chesapeake was his choice of where to engage the enemy, long before Washington had agreed to it.

A planning conference was soon set up held in Wethersfield, Connecticut; strategy was discussed by Rochambeau and de Chastellux for the French and Washington and Hamilton for the Americans. Because both sides shared different information about de Grasse's orders, Washington was at a disadvantage and somewhat out of his depth as a military planner. Rochambeau, with years more experience, was not easy to deal with and was determined not to attack New York City. About his dispatch to de Grasse to sail to the Chesapeake, one of his assistants said, "He mistrusts everyone and always believes that he sees himself surrounded by rogues and idiots."[32] Washington realized that without Rochambeau and now de Grasse he would lose the war and the British would regain their colonies. After the Wethersfield meetings, Washington appealed again to New England governors for troop levies, and he prepared to move his army out of the Hudson Valley, heading south toward New York City. Clinton had received word of this move from his spies. On June 10, the first brigade of

Rochambeau's army left Newport for a journey south that would be 750 miles to Yorktown. Washington had also written to de Grasse in early June asking him to sail north. Receiving this message while planning an attack on the island of Jamaica, de Grasse listened carefully to the bearer, an officer trusted by Washington, Allen McLane, who convinced him to turn north instead. De Grasse made his decision to sail for America. The die was cast.

"The Second Division"

Comte de Grasse, fifty-nine years old at this time, was a large, heavy-set man who was six feet two inches tall. He came from an old aristocratic family, went to a naval school at the age of eleven, had served in several military campaigns, and had been taken prisoner by the British for three months in 1740. He had served his country in the Indian Ocean, in the West Indies, in the Mediterranean, and in the Caribbean with Admiral d'Estaing, in 1778 commanding the seventy-four-gun *Intrépide*. Like Rochambeau, de Grasse was so experienced that General Washington was at a disadvantage. He understood that the French admiral was going to proceed the way he wanted. After his arrival at the Chesapeake Bay in August, de Grasse declared that he could only remain there until October 15 before returning to the West Indies. His first responsibility was his fleet, and his major concern was the British navy, particularly Admiral George Rodney, its most talented and aggressive of their many commodores. Rodney had been out of action for a year with an illness, but de Grasse feared his return.

The "Second Division" was composed of twenty ships of the line including de Grasse's flagship *Ville de Paris*. With 106 cannons, it was the largest warship in the world at that time. (Its successor was the *HMS Victory*, the flagship of Admiral Nelson, with 110 cannons in three rows on each side from bow to stern.) Each of de Grasse's ships of the line had seventy-four or more guns. Next in size were three frigates, each with three masts. These were smaller, faster, and more easily maneuvered with twenty-eight cannons in a single row on each side. One of the frigates was *La Diligente* under the command of Le Chevalier de Clouard. Its *chirurgien*-major (surgeon major) was Jean François Arnoux. He was ranked as an officer of the ship after the captain and five lieutenants. Two cutters, somewhat smaller than frigates, completed the military component of the fleet, which was charged with protecting 150 transports carrying soldiers to the French West Indies.

Jean François Arnoux, from Marseille, France, was a member of a family of surgeons that included his father before him as well as his relative Alexandré Arnoux and his son André from St. Paul de Vence. André had gone to Montreal in Canada in 1751 and assisted General Montcalm during the Seven Years' War. In the eighteenth century, surgeons learned their skills by apprenticing with their elders and by watching operations in hospitals. Anatomy was learned by carving up corpses. Training in France was considered among the best, along with Scotland. Historian David McCullough said, "Less well known but of great importance were the hundreds of young Americans who went to study medicine in France in the nineteenth century when Paris was the medical capital of the world..."[33] Other trainees went to the Netherlands' University at Leyden to study under Hermann Boerhaave, professor of medicine, botany, and chemistry. In the eighteenth century, the medical world rated physicians at the top and surgeons below them. The latter did the dirty work: lancing boils and letting blood. On board ship during battle they did amputations to save lives. On a ship of the line there would be a surgeon's mate to assist, but on a frigate the surgeon-major would have only the crew to assist him. On *La Diligente*, Arnoux was responsible for the well being of all, officers and crew.

During de Grasse's journey to the Western Hemisphere another squadron of six ships of the line joined the fleet at the Azores. The winds were fair during the passage south and the Island of Madeira was reached by April 2. From there the southeast trade winds sped the flotilla to Martinique, the biggest French naval base in the West Indies. No British ships had been sighted on the long journey until April 28 as the convoy approached Fort Royal, which guarded the magnificent Martinique Harbor. Admiral de Grasse was informed that the entrance was being blockaded by a British fleet under Admiral Sir Samuel Hood, who had been waiting for their arrival. Hood was considered one of the best British admirals of the day and had served under Rodney in the Seven Years' War. His squadron consisted of twenty ships of the line, only slightly less than the twenty-six of de Grasse. A battle seemed certain to follow, and the British were the better sailors.

In the first skirmish, the British ships maintained excellent order while the French ship *Vaillant* suffered heavy damage from being shelled by four enemy ships for two hours. The next day the two fleets tried to outmaneuver each other, to no avail. On the following day, de Grasse discovered Hood was withdrawing; he tried but failed to catch him, and thence headed for the harbor of Fort Royal. Upon anchoring he summoned all his captains for a dressing down for poor performance in obeying signals. On the next day, three hundred French infantry were unloaded from the 150 transports. The convoy had successfully carried out the first part of its mission. The fleet needed time to rest and replenish its supplies, which were running low.

Off again on a cruise, de Grasse captured the British island of Tobago on June 1 and came close to engaging Rodney who sailed away at night. Two weeks later he sailed to Granada, Puerto Rico, and anchored in Cape François (Cape Haitien) on July 16. It was here that he received a letter from Rochambeau urging him to sail for Chesapeake Bay and to bring funds—2.5 million livres were requested. Weighing anchor on August 5, the French fleet picked up the money in Havana, Cuba, and proceeded north with transports carrying 3,500 soldiers and artillery, the Agénois, Gatinais, and Touraine regiments under the Marquis de Saint-Simon. Three small British warships were captured en route before the fleet anchored on the evening of August 28, three leagues from the roadstead of Chesapeake Bay "in calm water 13 to 18 fathoms deep with a sand bottom."[34] The admiral had detached four ships of his fleet to sail ahead to clear the area of unfriendly ships: the *Glorieux*, the *Aigrette*, the *Diligente*, and the boat *Loyalist* (the first was a ship of the line, the second and third frigates). They had shut off the James River to prevent the retreat of Cornwallis to North Carolina. The Marquis Saint-Simon's regiments were put ashore on September 2.

Admiral de Grasse from his flagship *Ville de Paris* looked out over twenty-eight ships of the line, four frigates, fifteen thousand sailors, eight hundred marines, and three regiments of soldiers all devoted to the destruction of the British army at Yorktown. Except for Lafayette's American troops, the armies of Washington and Rochambeau had not yet arrived. The "second division" that both generals had requested almost a year ago at Hartford was in place and ready for duty.

When de Grasse arrived he also received a word of warning, a report from Washington that a British fleet of twenty-four ships under command of Admiral Graves had left New York and was in the vicinity of Maryland and Virginia. De Grasse was put on alert to leave on short notice to engage with him.*

Chesapeake Bay

Chesapeake Bay had become the focal point for the armies of General Washington and Rochambeau and the navy of Admiral de Grasse, who had come together against their enemy under the command of Charles, Earl of Cornwallis, second in command to Sir Henry Clinton, who had succeeded Sir William Howe after the Battle of Saratoga in 1777. These two British ranking officers, Clinton and Cornwallis, had a difficult relationship with each other. Although Clinton was the senior, Cornwallis acted as though he did not accept that fact and communicated directly with Lord George Germain in London, secretary of state for the American colonies. This situation was made worse because of the incompetent and aging Admiral Arbuthnot who refused to cooperate with Clinton and, at age sixty-nine, in 1781, had to be replaced by Admiral Thomas Graves. Graves turned out to be a poor choice as well, being very cautious about engaging the enemy. This complicated command structure and the length of time it took—two months—to communicate with Whitehall in London resulted in decisions that were eventually fatal to the British effort to put down their rebellion in the States.

To step back a year in time to May 1780, Clinton decided to move a part of the army south to attack Charleston, South Carolina. In a brilliant move he besieged the city, defeated Benjamin Lincoln, captured or killed four thousand Americans, and established an important base for invasion of the southern states. When the victory at Charleston was complete, he turned over command to Cornwallis and sailed back to New York, the principal headquarters of the British forces. Clinton was described as aloof, resentful, and self-reproachful. His wife had died and he was a lonely man. For long periods of time he never wrote to Cornwallis, who took it upon himself to be the commander in the south.

General Cornwallis came from an old aristocratic family. He attended Eton College and at eighteen became an ensign in the Grenadier Guards. He rose in ranks to be a lieutenant colonel in his regiment, and upon the death of

---

* See the Battle of the Capes, page 83.

his father he became a member of the House of Lords. He had fought in America earlier in the Battles of Long Island and Fort Lee in 1776, at the Battle of Princeton, where Washington eluded him, and also at Brandywine and Germantown. Exactly the opposite of Clinton in temperament, he was aggressive as a military leader and very successful throughout the south in the early part of the effort in 1780 and 1781. The problem lay in the fact that Clinton and Cornwallis were acting on different premises and seldom talked to each other. Clinton urged that Charleston be secured, followed by a slow advance north up the coast to North Carolina and Virginia so the advance could be supported by the navy. Instead, Cornwallis went inland in South Carolina, had a victory at Camden but gradually wore his troops out and lengthened his supply lines to such an extent that American General Nathaniel Greene could defeat him. On April 13, 1781, after defeat at Guilford Courthouse, Cornwallis finally wrote to Clinton in New York: "My present understanding sits heavy on my mind. I have experienced the distress and dangers of marching some hundreds of miles, in a country chiefly hostile, without one active or useful friend; without intelligence, and without communication with any part of the country."[35] His army was depleted with sick or wounded soldiers, many without shoes and worn down with fatigue. He had lost 1,500 of his 3,200 men. He began to look for reinforcements from Europe. He was in the dark, he told Clinton, as to plans for the summer, but hoped the Chesapeake would become the seat of war. Assuming that Britain still controlled the seas, he made a plan to move to a position where he could be easily supplied by his navy. The best place seemed to be a peninsula between the York and James Rivers in Virginia. Over the next few months more fighting occurred, but Cornwallis moved north into Virginia. By the first of August, Cornwallis had set up camp in the little town called Yorktown to await supply from Admiral Graves, then in charge of the British fleet. It was a perfect mooring, with deep water and protection for the British fleet to maneuver should the French attack. Unknown to the British, however, at the exact time that Cornwallis and his army were settling in to Yorktown, Rochambeau received word from de Grasse that he would sail for the Chesapeake to position his fleet at the mouth of the bay, effectively trapping Cornwallis without any chance of his escape by water. Washington immediately instructed Lafayette, who controlled American forces in Virginia, to close the gate on land, locking the English into prison on a hill called Yorktown. With the two armies then on the way, escape over land would be impos-

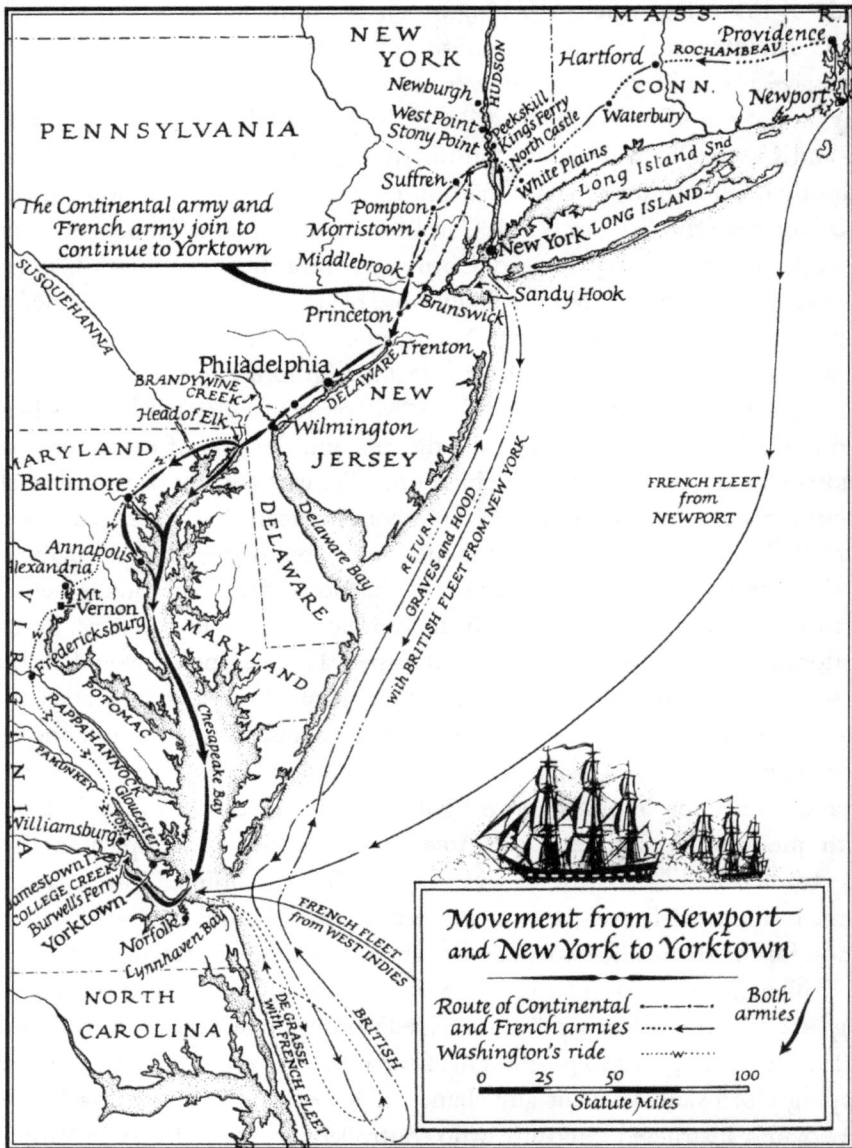

The Road to Yorktown, 1781. Movement of the armies and navies.

sible, as would escape over sea except in the unlikely event that Admiral Graves could defeat the huge fleet of Admiral de Grasse.

From Newport to Yorktown

Soon after the news of de Grasse's departure from France reached America, both Generals Rochambeau and Washington prepared to move their armies. On June 10, the first brigade of French troops left Newport for the long 750-mile overland march to the south. Their destination was not revealed, as it was most important for Clinton in New York to believe that an attack would be made on the main part of the British forces there. Indeed, General Washington still wanted the city to be the intended target, and he arranged that a letter to a subordinate that indicated such a target be leaked to a spy. The departure of the French from Newport was an emotional moment. They had been well received there by the local population and many were sorry to see them depart. The six thousand men had added greatly to the economy of Newport for the whole year that they were there. "As the brilliantly uniformed troops dressed ranks, crowds lining the streets waved their hats and cheered and threw kisses as they began to march to the docks, where they embarked for Providence."[36] (Newport is on an island in Narragansett Bay.) Rochambeau, after a year of inactivity, could not wait to leave. He had the honor of leading the cream of the French military—the Soissonnaise and Bourbonnais regiments, with which he had fought in the Seven Years' War—along with the distinguished Saintonge and Deux-Ponts regiments. He fully expected another great victory, and the prizes and awards that went with it, for the French army of that time.

In Providence, the army was divided into four divisions for the overland march. The going was difficult, especially for the artillery, because of very poor roads. It took two weeks to reach Hartford, Connecticut, where they set up camp for two days of rest and repair. (The heavy cannons were to be shipped directly to Yorktown later by a part of the French fleet.) The route from Hartford went to Farmington, Connecticut, then to Newtown, Connecticut (much as Route 84 does today). At Newtown, Rochambeau heard from Washington that he was on the march and hoped to meet up with him soon. He wanted the first brigade of French to be in Bedford, New York, on July 2, and from there go to New Castle, to Philipsburg at White Plains, and finally to Dobbs Ferry on the Hudson River by July 6. The next day the two armies camped side by side and Rochambeau put on a formal review for Washington and all his officers. The Americans reciprocated on the following day. The French had traveled 220 miles in eleven days and needed a rest.

Perhaps to indulge Washington, Rochambeau agreed that the two generals make a careful study of the area, spending days in the saddle. In the third week of July, a reconnaissance in force was made, after which both concluded that with five thousand French troops and somewhat fewer Americans, an attack on Clinton's fourteen thousand troops, all British veterans behind fortified lines protected by the British navy in the Hudson and East Rivers, was doomed to failure. Washington was finally satisfied to turn south to Yorktown, but both generals agreed to cross the Hudson to the west side and to pass by New York City close to the river in a way to convince Clinton that an invasion of Staten Island was the target. This would keep the British general from sending reinforcements to Cornwallis in Virginia. On the day—August 1—that Washington decided to change his target to Virginia, he also learned from Lafayette that Cornwallis had moved into the Yorktown peninsula. Could he get there in time to keep him there? This was his major concern. On August 14, while still on route, he learned by letter from de Grasse that he was sailing for the Chesapeake with twenty-nine warships and three thousand troops. Washington had less than two months to concentrate three armies of about twelve thousand men (including de Grasse's soldiers), and he was still several hundred miles away.

The armies crossed the Hudson River at Kingsbridge and moved into New Jersey. Washington brought along landing craft to maintain the fiction of an invasion of Staten Island. Of the entire trip south, crossing the Hudson was the most vulnerable time for them; amazingly, Clinton did nothing to interfere. No British warship appeared. Clinton, believing that New York City was the target, did not want to provoke an action north of the city where he was not prepared. It was another error in judgment, and it would not be the last.

The French, in full dress uniforms, followed by the American armies three days later, paraded through the nation's capital, Philadelphia, on August 30. Rochambeau was feted at the home of Robert Morris, financier of the revolution. It was in Philadelphia that Washington learned that Admiral de Grasse had departed from Chesapeake Bay. "I am distressed beyond expression to know that Admiral de Grasse had departed from Chesapeake Bay."[37] As it turned out, the British squadron under Admiral Graves had appeared from New York, and the French admiral wasted no time to engage it. Leaving four ships of the line and three frigates including *La Diligente* in the Chesapeake Bay to control the entrance of the York and James Rivers, he took his fleet to sea to attack the enemy.

Known as the Battle of the Capes—between Cape Charles and Cape Henry, lasting from September 5 to September 10—it was the definitive sea battle of the Yorktown campaign. Had de Grasse lost, the British navy would have relieved Cornwallis or re-supplied him, and the final outcome for Washington and Rochambeau would have been very different. The battle became only a partial engagement. Only one ship, a British frigate, was lost, scuttled to avoid its capture. Admiral Graves failed to attack de Grasse's fleet as it emerged one by one from the Chesapeake, losing an advantage he never recovered. Graves' caution and lethargy gave his opponent a big advantage, but in the light winds the fleets drifted south and de Grasse's much larger number of ships were not able to engage any further. Finally Graves withdrew in the night and sailed north back to New York, much to Washington's relief. De Grasse returned to the Chesapeake again, sealing the trap on Cornwallis.

On the same day that de Grasse returned, a second much smaller French fleet under Count de Barras arrived from Newport, having successfully avoided contact with Graves returning to New York. De Barras, with eight ships of the line, two frigates, and eighteen transports, carried the heavy siege cannons that could not be brought over land and were vital to a successful, speedy siege of Yorktown.

With this good news, the two armies proceeded south from Philadelphia. They had halted while de Grasse was out at sea. As travel by water in ships was much speedier than marching overland, for travel to the Yorktown peninsula Washington had planned to board his army onto boats at the northern point of the Chesapeake Bay where the river Elk empties into the bay. He put in a call for all available boats but few turned up. Admiral de Grasse helped by assigning four ships of the line and three frigates to the effort, but because of their deep draft they could not navigate north of Baltimore, and only smaller boats could go up the Elk and back with a full load. Most of the army had to walk the entire way to Virginia. Only two thousand soldiers were ferried south, principally the grenadiers and chasseurs with small cannons. The trip was made in bad weather and took eighteen days.

Battle of the Virginia Capes, 5 September 1781. Oil on canvas by v. Zveg, 1962, depicting the French fleet (at left), commanded by Vice Admiral the Comte de Grasse, engaging the British fleet (at right) under Rear Admiral Sir Thomas Graves off the mouth of Chesapeake.

The first units to arrive in the Yorktown area were the four regiments under Saint-Simon, which had come with Admiral de Grasse. On September 1, they were put ashore on the north side of the peninsula to make sure Cornwallis could not escape. Lafayette, with American soldiers, was on the south side. The main armies from the north arrived after mid-September.

A Council of War

After their arrival in Yorktown it was essential that Generals Washington and Rochambeau take council with Admiral de Grasse. To that end they and their senior staff, including Chastellux, Knox, and, importantly, the French engineer Duportail, set off on September 18 on a sailing vessel sent by de Grasse on the sixty-mile journey down the James River out the Chesapeake Bay to where the flagship *Ville de Paris* was anchored. Washington must have been impressed when he saw for the first time more than thirty ships of the line headed by the enormous *Ville de Paris*, the largest warship in the world. The party was piped aboard "with great ceremony and military naval parade."[38] "The admiral is a remarkable man for size, appearance, and plainness of address," remarked a witness.[39] He was in fact taller than George Washington and considerably heavier.

After introductions and formalities, Washington put the two questions of greatest importance to de Grasse: Was the admiral bound by a definite date of departure of the fleet? And if Saint-Simon's troops were obliged to leave ahead of the fleet, would the main naval force remain in the Chesapeake to cover the siege against Cornwallis? De Grasse responded to the first that his instructions were to leave on October 15, but he would, on his own, stretch that to the end of that month, giving two armies six weeks' time to obtain the British surrender. As for Saint-Simon's troops, they could be counted upon until the fleet's departure. He also promised Washington 1,800 to 2,000 more men, and more heavy cannon (but was short on powder). The six-hour visit was soon over, and the generals took their leave for a long trip back to their armies upriver. Washington had one fright. When arriving back at camp he heard that a rumor of a British squadron coming had persuaded de Grasse to weigh anchor again and sail toward New York to engage it. Rochambeau immediately wrote a message to de Grasse: "The plan to go to New York, of which you ask our counsel, seems

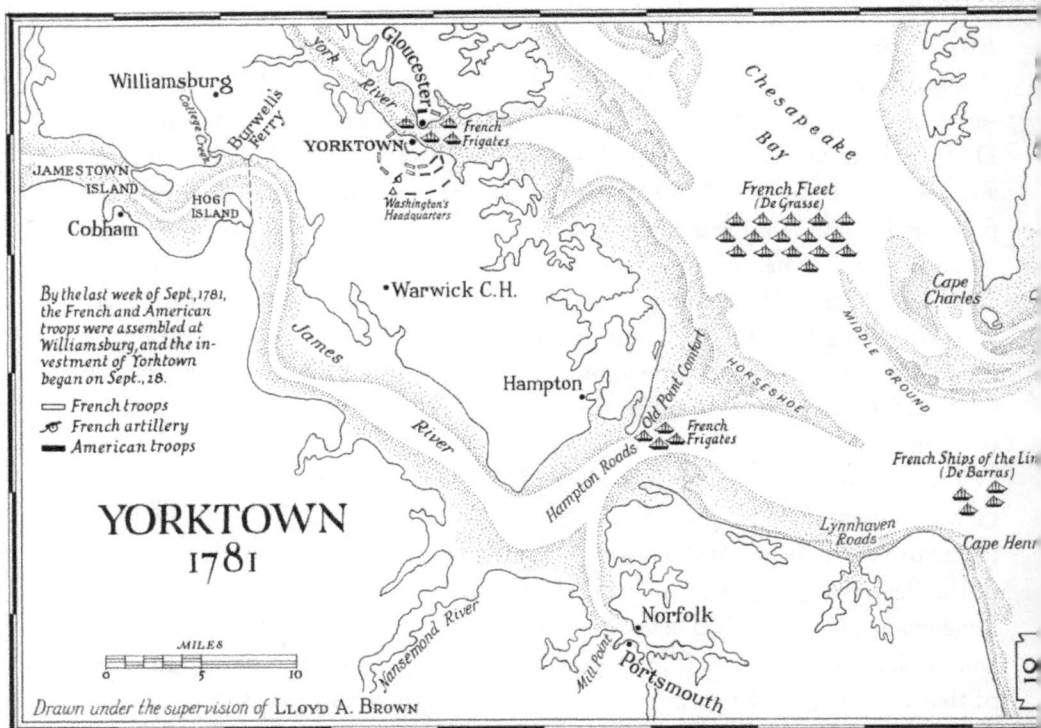

The disposition of the French fleet in September and October 1781 during the siege of Yorktown. The smaller frigates were close to the battle, while the larger ships of the line were stationed to block any attempt at rescue by a British fleet.

to us a matter of the greatest hazard" since the British would likely come to rescue Cornwallis and "would be able in the night to pass without your seeing them." Upon reflection, de Grasse replied on September 27: "The plans I had suggested for getting underway, while the most brilliant and glorious, did not appear to fulfill the aims we had in view. Accordingly it was decided that the major part of the fleet should proceed to anchor in York River."[40] Washington was relieved that the whole plan was not ruined at the last moment. A French admiral had been persuaded by a French general to alter his plan. It will never be known if the admiral would have been persuaded by Washington alone. Washington and Rochambeau would now institute their attack on Yorktown, which they had been dreaming about for a year. It was September 28, 1781. They had only one month before de Grasse's departure.

The Siege, September 28 to October 19, 1781

Inside the British perimeter at Yorktown, Lord Cornwallis had nearly 7,500 soldiers, including a Hessian regiment plus eight hundred to nine hundred marines. Many of the troops were in poor condition due to the arduous campaigning in spring and summer in the Carolinas and Virginia. They were also short of senior officers who had been killed in combat.

Confronting these were about sixteen thousand American and French soldiers led by the best and most experienced officers, giving them more than a two-to-one advantage. The French commanders in particular were veterans of fixed-place battles. They were Major Generals Saint-Simon, Baron Vioménil, Comte de Vioménil, Chastellux, and Duportail. The plan of attack was to be a siege, followed by onslaught and capture. Rochambeau himself over his career had been involved in fourteen sieges, and Duportail, the chief engineer, was thoroughly trained in the use of the tactic, having studied in engineering school in France the ritual for sieges set down by French Marshal Sébastien Le Prestre de Vauban seventy-five years earlier under Louis XIV, the Sun King. Duportail had laid out on paper the siege lines and artillery positions to be used by both French and Americans, and later supervised the digging of trenches approaching enemy lines in parallel, zigzag formation in preparation for the assault. No American officer had ever taken part in a siege, although Alexander Hamilton had read books about the tactics.

On the morning of September 28, the two armies marched out of camp for twelve miles to take up positions around the perimeter of land in the town where Cornwallis was situated. The part on the York River was covered by some of de Grasse's fleet. From north to south on the land side were the French regiments of Saint-Simon, Comte de Vioménil, Baron de Vioménil, and behind them French artillery; the American sector to the south of the French were the regiments of Baron von Steuben, Generals James Clinton, Benjamin Lincoln, Lafayette, Thomas Nelson, and behind them, the artillery of Henry Knox. And behind this were the headquarters of Rochambeau and Washington. Alexander Hamilton, the general's aide, had asked for a command position and had been assigned to attack Redoubt Ten. With the armies in place the siege began.

In preparation for the battle the British had cleared the approach to the town of all vegetation, creating as one soldier said, "a flat sandy plain that could be swept by English cannon."[41] The defenders had surrounded the town with a line of earthworks that connected ten redoubts (small forts). Numbers nine and ten were in the front of the line on the south where the terrain favored the attacker. Sixty-five cannon were mounted along the defense perimeter, all of which were less than eighteen pounders. The French had much larger cannons, thanks to Rochambeau's foresight. Cornwallis tried to raise morale by telling his men that the enemy had fewer men, that they had no siege artillery, and that the French would soon leave. All of these assumptions would prove false.

The key to the American and French success was in the ritual of the siege as laid out by Duportail and carried out by both American and French engineers and sappers. The first trench, about six hundred yards from the enemy line, was dug perpendicular to the south side of the fortified town—the weak side. The second trench was to be dug parallel to the first after it had been completed about three hundred yards from the enemy. Each of the trenches would be ten feet wide, four feet deep, and about two miles long—a major excavation that afforded protection as well as access. Dug by sappers, largely at night, with pickaxes—Rochambeau had come with four thousand axes—dirt from the excavation was thrown onto fascines in front of the parallels, forming parapets. The battery locations were dug out and connected to the parallel by other trenches. Heavy cannon could then be brought in close to the enemy— within three hundred yards—without being fired upon. Smaller trenches connected the two large ones and were dug in zigzag paths toward the redoubts nine and ten (see diagram), the capture of which would assure victory to the attacker.

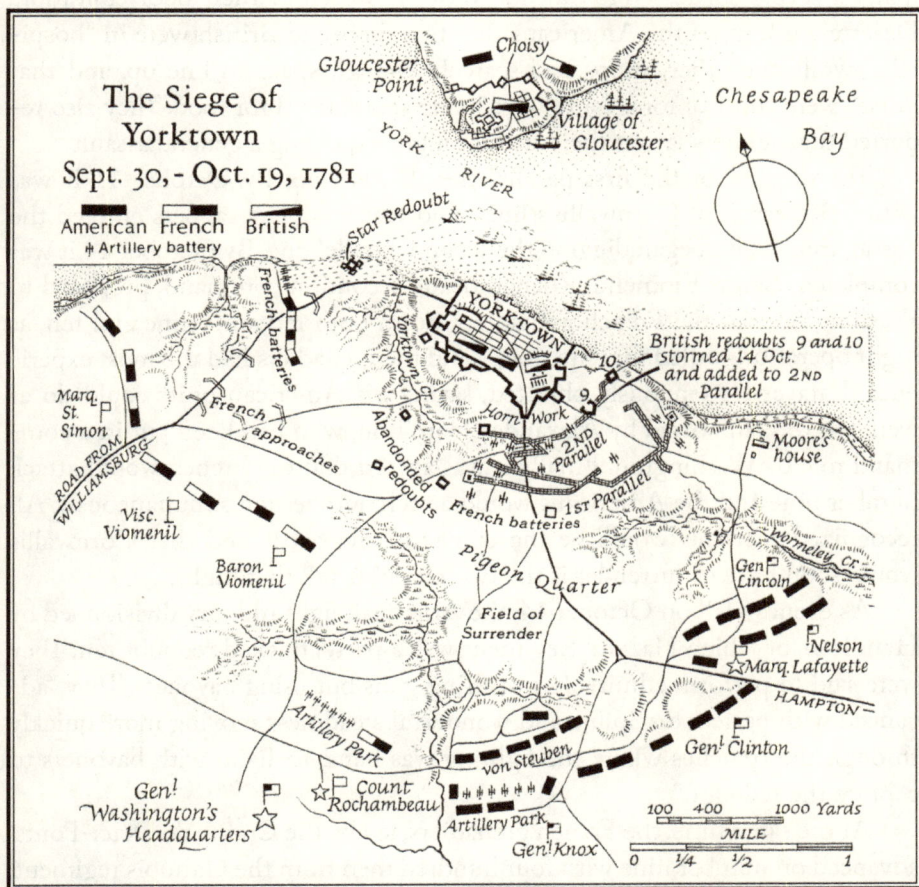

The Siege of Yorktown
Sept. 30, - Oct. 19, 1781

American French British
+ Artillery battery

Gloucester Point
Choisy
Village of Gloucester

Chesapeake Bay

YORK RIVER

Star Redoubt

French batteries

YORKTOWN

10

British redoubts 9 and 10 stormed 14 Oct. and added to 2ND Parallel

9

Horn Work

2ND Parallel

Moore's house

Marq. St. Simon

French approaches

Abandoned redoubts

French batteries

1ST Parallel

Wormeley Cr.

ROAD FROM WILLIAMSBURG

Visc. Viomenil

Baron Viomenil

Pigeon Quarter

Field of Surrender

Gen! Lincoln

Nelson
Marq. Lafayette

HAMPTON

Artillery Park

von Steuben

Gen! Clinton

Gen! Washington's Headquarters

Count Rochambeau

Artillery Park

Gen! Knox

100 400 1000 Yards
MILE
0 1/4 1/2 1

Positions of the three armies during the siege. The attack on British redoubts nine and ten was the critical event in the battle.

Beginning on October 1, the British artillery fired every day and continued at night. In the midst of this the American and French sappers were digging a trench toward them. American General Anthony Wayne said, "The reduction of Cornwallis's army was going to require time and much bloodshed, for it was absurd to think that he would tacitly surrender seven thousand troops without many a severe sortie."[42] He did not know, however, of their poor condition. Deserters informed the Americans that two thousand British were in "hospitals," while the other troops had scarcely enough space to line up, and that horses were short of forage and were being slaughtered for food. They also reported that soldiers lay on their arms at night expecting a general assault.

The digging of the first parallel trench went on. By October 11 it was within 360 yards of Cornwallis's lines, and von Steuben's sappers entered the zigzag trench and began digging the second parallel one. By October 14 it was completed. Baron Vioménil, Rochambeau's second in command, proposed to Washington that the French grenadiers storm both redoubts nine and ten, as night operations called for elite troops and the grenadiers had the most experience. Lafayette strenuously objected, saying his American units could do as well. He was supported by Alexander Hamilton, who had been put in a command role by Washington. Finally it was agreed that the French would attack number nine and the Americans would attack number ten simultaneously. All recognized that this would be the climax of the battle and that Cornwallis would soon have to surrender if the two redoubts fell that night.

As evening fell on October 14, the American light military division led by Hamilton, of which Hazen's Regiment was a part, attacked redoubt ten. They were said to perform admirably, not firing guns but using bayonets. They "advanced with perfect discipline and wonderful steadiness moving more quickly through the trenches where the fighting was hand-to-hand with bayonets to capture the redoubt."[43]

At the same time, the French grenadiers, led by the Comte de Deux-Ponts, advanced on number nine with four hundred men from the Gatinois regiment, many with long storming pikes. The French had waited for more support while under intense British fire until urged on by Rochambeau himself. In this firefight forty-six men were lost and sixty-two were wounded; the wounded included six officers, one being a captain whose leg was shot off. All wounds tended to be serious, and the most serious ones were almost always fatal. Surgeons from de Grasse's ships were there to perform amputations quickly, which helped to save lives. One of these surgeons, Jean François Arnoux from *La Diligente*, was himself wounded in the knee during the battle.

By the morning of October 15, the allies had secured all the British redoubts and began to fire their heavy cannons that had been dragged into the trenches. At this close range, no more than five hundred yards from Yorktown, this bombardment meant instant death to any unprotected British soldier. Cornwallis wrote to Clinton in New York that day: "My situation now becomes very critical. We dare not show a gun to their old batteries."[44] "The safety of the place is, therefore, so precarious that I cannot recommend that a fleet and army should run the risk in endeavoring to save us."[45] He knew the game was up. The bombardment continued unabated. On October 17 it began again and was even more devastating.

That morning, Cornwallis sent a white flag of truce over to his enemy. He had seen enough slaughter of his men and informed Clinton of his decision to surrender. "Under all these circumstances, I thought it would have been wanton and inhuman to the last degree to sacrifice the lives of this small body of gallant soldiers, who had ever behaved with such fidelity and courage, by exposing them to an assault, which from the numbers and precautions of the enemy could not fail to succeed. I therefore proposed to capitulate."[46] On that same day a rescue fleet from General Clinton sailed from New York, unbeknownst to Cornwallis, only to turn around and return upon finding the French fleet in control of the Chesapeake Bay. It was too small and too late.

The British officer bearing the white flag carried a message for General Washington. Blindfolded, he was taken to the general's tent where he handed it to him. It read:

> Sir, I propose a cessation of hostilities for twenty-four hours, and that two officers may be appointed by each side, to meet at Mr. Moore's house [a mile or so downriver] to settle terms for the surrender of the posts at York and Gloucester. I have the honor to be,
>
> Cornwallis[47]

Although the British officer carrying the white flag was given protection, the heaviest fire yet was pouring on the enemy. At 2:00 pm Washington replied to Cornwallis's proposal, "I wish previously to the Meeting of Commissioners, that Your Lordship's proposals in writing, may be sent to the American Lines, for which Purpose, a Suspension of Hostilities during two Hours from Delivery of the Letter will be granted."[48]

Cornwallis replied at 4:30 pm with terms not acceptable to Washington, but the latter permitted hostilities to be suspended until the signing of an agreement, taking the small risk that the British would take advantage of the delay. The two commissions met the next day, on the afternoon of October 18, to settle the matter. Washington had given them until early on the morning of October 19. At about 11:00 am that day the text of the articles of surrender was signed by Cornwallis. To this Washington added, "done in the trenches before Yorktown, in Virginia, October 19, 1781" and signed "G. Washington."[49] Then the French commander signed "Le Comte de Rochambeau" and his naval colleague added "Le Comte de Barras, En mon nom + celui du comte de Grasse," as the latter was sick and had to remain on the *Ville de Paris*. The battle was officially over, less than thirty days after the first shots were fired.

The terms of surrender were tough, but not more so than could have been expected. In summary, "The captive troops are to march out with shouldered arms, colors cased and drums beating a British or German march, and to ground their arms at a place assigned for the purpose."[50] Officers were allowed to keep their sidearms and personal property; generals and high ranking officers could go on parole to England or New York (Lord Cornwallis chose to be sent to London by ship, after refusing to attend the ceremony that day saying he was ill); marines and seamen were to be prisoners of war of the French navy; land forces would remain in the United States, to be sent to Virginia, Maryland, and Pennsylvania in regiments with rations equal to American soldiers, to be kept in detention until the end of the war.

The British army lost the use of eight thousand soldiers and marines. Five hundred and fifty-six were killed or wounded, and the balance were taken prisoner. Two thousand of the prisoners were sick, having been with Cornwallis's army since May 1780 in the Carolinas with inadequate food and supplies. While large, these losses were only a third of their military might in the Western Hemisphere. The responsibility for guarding these prisoners fell in part to Hazen's Regiment, which it carried out for ten months at prison camps in Lancaster, York, and Reading, Pennsylvania. In November 1782, the regiment moved to winter quarters in Pompton, New Jersey, joining the rest of Washington's main army on the Hudson River at Fishkill and West Point.

The French lost 389 men, of which ninety-eight soldiers and officers were killed, the rest wounded, primarily in the assault on redoubt nine. Americans suffered the fewest casualties: ten officers and 289 men killed or wounded.

On the afternoon of October 19, the British army marched out of Yorktown to surrender their arms. Leading them was General Charles O'Hara of the Coldstream Guards, who explained to General Washington that Lord Cornwallis was ill and offered his sword to him. Washington declined to receive it, indicating that he should present it to General Benjamin Lincoln, his second-in-command. Lincoln held it for a symbolic moment and returned it to O'Hara, pointing to the field where all British arms were to be laid down in piles before marching on to captivity. Cornwallis had refused to appear, which outraged the French and Americans, but this abstention did not damage his career. He sailed safely back to England and was to serve his country again, with distinction, in India.

De Grasse Departs Yorktown

General Washington had hoped to persuade Admiral de Grasse to ferry his army to Charleston to besiege the British still in control of that major port city in the south. However, he replied that his orders would not permit that diversion and that he would be sailing for the West Indies. He left behind a ship of the line and two frigates. One frigate, *Hermione*, in February of 1782 would take Baron de Vioménil and eighteen officers back to France; the other, *La Diligente*, would run aground on Cape Henry on its way to Boston to take on some ammunition that had been left there. The ship foundered with twenty-four sailors losing their lives. Arnoux had earlier left the ship to help the wounded in Yorktown, and having been wounded himself, he was not on board. Comte de Rochambeau wrote movingly of this tragic incident:

> The latter vessel was run ashore, through the awkwardness of her pilot. I mention the circumstance, as it affords me an opportunity of rendering justice to the remarkable courage evinced by her captain [Monsieur de Clouard] on this unfortunate occasion; he remained three days up to his middle in water and could not be induced to withdraw until he had saved everything on board his frigate; he was shortly thereafter attacked with a violent fever, which had been nearly his death. This brave officer had always been unfortunate; for this was the third time he had been wrecked, and he has since perished with "La Pegrouse," in his voyage round the world.[51]

De Grasse departed the Chesapeake Bay with his fleet on November 4 to defend French interest in the Caribbean, knowing that more than one British fleet was active there and that the war between the two countries continued. Upon his departure it was very obvious to Washington that the British navy was again in command of American waters, and that the victory at Yorktown had not ended the war. De Grasse's fleet arrived off Fort Royal on Martinique on November 25 to refit and restock the warships during the holiday season. In January, the admiral set off again to attack the British, capturing St. Kitts. He then had a confrontation with Admiral Hood, which was indecisive, before having the misfortune in April to engage with the aggressive Admiral George Rodney, who was back at sea from illness the previous year. In this engagement, known at the Battle of the Saints, de Grasse had thirty-five ships of the line escorting one hundred transports loaded with soldiers. They were sailing off the island of Guadeloupe when Rodney set upon his capital ships. He used a new tactic the French had never seen before, which entailed breaking through the line of their ships at a ninety-degree angle instead of engaging at a parallel. The surprise to the French and superior gunnery of the British resulted in breaking the French line at three points, their loss of seven ships of the line, one frigate, and the capture of de Grasse himself. The transports escaped but Admiral Rodney had another victory to add to his lifetime record. De Grasse was exchanged two years later, regaining his freedom.

It is interesting to note that a student of this new tactic, not in the action himself, was young Captain Horatio Nelson, who heard about it from afar while cruising between Cape Cod and Boston, in search of American or French shipping in that area. He would use it much later when, as admiral of the fleet at the Battles of the Nile in 1798 and Trafalgar in 1805, he destroyed a large part of the French navy. The British navy was not seriously threatened again for over a century.[52]

The First Meeting

It was either on the battlefield near the end of the siege or shortly thereafter that the French-speaking surgeon Jean François Arnoux of *La Diligente* first met Pierre and Jean Chartier, soldiers in Hazen's Regiment, who also spoke French as their native tongue. Arnoux, who was born in Marseille in 1752, was a few years older than the brothers. Having been assigned ashore during the siege to help French soldiers wounded in battle, he was most likely in the trenches near redoubt nine when he was wounded in the knee. The Chartiers, as a part of Hazen's Regiment, were attacking redoubt ten and suffered far fewer casualties. While recovering from his wound, Arnoux remained with the French army in Virginia, and a friendship with the Chartiers could have developed before Hazen's Regiment left on its next assignment of taking prisoners to Pennsylvania. Arnoux may have been curious upon finding soldiers in the American army who spoke his language, and he probably knew that a relative of his family, André Arnoux, had also been a surgeon who had been located in Montreal in 1751 and had served in the Seven Years' War with General Montcalm in Canada. In talking with the Chartier brothers he may have discovered that their grandfather Jean Chartier had known André Arnoux as well.

The Chartier brothers remained with Hazen's Regiment for the next eighteen months until it was disbanded in 1783 (see Part III). The whereabouts of Arnoux in this period is not known. None of the French soldiers nor the French-speaking Canadians were welcome back in Canada while the British were still at war with France, and even after the peace treaty of 1783 the French-speaking Canadians who fought at Yorktown were very suspect for several years. It is thought that Arnoux may have reached St. Antoine in 1785 to visit the Chartier family who were then living there.

With the departure of the French navy from the Chesapeake Bay on November 4, 1781, the American militias left Yorktown as well, most to join Washington's main army on the Hudson River south of West Point. The rest were assigned to General Nathaniel Greene, whose task was to recapture Charleston, South Carolina, without any help from the French navy. The British army remained in Charleston and of course New York City. Their navy controlled the seas along the east coast. The war was certainly not over.

The French Army in America, 1782–1783

General Rochambeau's army left Yorktown to winter in Williamsburg, Virginia, up the peninsula. They had suffered relatively few casualties and were still five thousand men strong with the same leadership—no important French officer was lost in the battle. The question remained: How could they be useful to Washington without the presence of the French navy? The winter lay ahead with little to do. Unlike at Newport in 1780–1781, they did not get along well with the Virginians. The French officers who had been given bonuses for their efforts at Yorktown (as was the French custom) had no place to spend their money and wanted to return to France. In the two years the French army was in the United States, no more than three hundred soldiers left to live there, and very few learned to speak English. Only one left to establish a commercial career.

In a strategic sense, nothing had changed since 1780 except that Cornwallis's army no longer existed as a threat. However, because of the victory at Yorktown, American morale had greatly improved while British morale had greatly declined. The parliament in London began to wonder if it was worth the cost in men and money to keep the American colony. It took another year to convince a stubborn George III that a peace treaty should be sought and the war ended.

Rochambeau's army remained in Williamsburg from November 1781 to July 1782, almost nine months. During this time the general visited families throughout Virginia, including Thomas Jefferson at Monticello in the spring. That summer a long, slow march northward began with Boston as its destination. There were long layovers in Baltimore and Philadelphia before circling north of New York to avoid the British, who were no longer interested in fighting but would not depart. Then it was on to Hartford, Providence, and finally Boston. Rochambeau himself had left his army in Philadelphia in January 1783 to take a ship back to France to receive honors and congratulations from his king. From Boston his army was shipped to the Caribbean for duty with a new leader. The last French soldiers to leave the United States departed from Wilmington, Delaware, on May 11, 1783.

In 1791, Rochambeau was promoted to a marshal of France, the highest rank of the country. But times were changing; the ancien régime had been deposed only to be replaced by a reign of terror under Robespierre. Only the latter's death saved the marshal from the guillotine. In 1803, Napoleon made him "grand officer of the Legion d'Honneur." In 1807, at the age of eighty-two, he died a natural death, surviving George Washington by eight years.

While the French and American armies fought no battles against Great Britain in 1782 and 1783, French and British navies were in combat in the West Indies, and diplomats on all sides began to negotiate for a peace treaty. In England, when Prime Minister Lord North received news of Cornwallis's defeat at Yorktown, he said, "Oh God, it is all over!" Yet George III absolutely refused to change his policy, accusing opponents of being "disloyal subjects."[53]

Opinion in his country was changing, however, and at the end of February 1782 the House of Commons voted against continuing the war, authorizing the monarch to make peace with the colonies. A month later, Lord North and his ministers resigned, including Lord Germain, who had been in overall charge of conducting the war. Finally, after a year the stubborn king announced on February 14, 1783, that hostilities had ceased between Great Britain, France, Spain, Holland, and the United States of America. After he received this proclamation from George III—no longer his king—General Washington on April 18 announced in general orders to his army that all fighting would cease. It was exactly eight years since Paul Revere had warned the people of Lexington and Concord, Massachusetts, that the Redcoats were coming and they had fired "the shot heard around the world."

An armistice had begun, but a peace treaty, the Treaty of Paris, was not agreed to or signed until September, five months later. During these months the Congress of the United States decided to send all the troops home, largely unpaid, except for a few to watch over the British garrison in New York. British troops in Charleston and Savannah had been evacuated by the British navy, and only in New York City and Long Island did any remain.

Meanwhile in Paris, Benjamin Franklin, the ambassador, had been joined by John Adams and John Jay for the United States to negotiate the treaty. They were surprised when the British proposed that the opening sentence of Article I read, "His Britannic Majesty acknowledges the said United States... to be free, sovereign, and independent states."[54] This was a surprise to the French as well, who were a party to these negotiations. The three Americans skillfully managed to obtain virtually everything they wanted, even one clause that the French opposed concerning fishing rights off Canada. Vergennes for the French had been secretly informing the British that it opposed many American claims regarding boundaries and fisheries, and had wanted to reclaim some parts of Canada that the French had lost to the British in 1763. In that effort he was unsuccessful. At the end, the ever-practical Franklin succeeded in persuading Vergennes to grant the United States a loan of another six million livres.

On November 25, 1783, known as Evacuation Day, the remaining British troops marched out of New York City and Long Island. With them went many of the Tory families who had been there during the long occupation of nine years—longer than any in the country. Some went to England, and many went to the part of Canada called Acadia (now Nova Scotia) where in the principal city, Halifax, the British had a large naval base in the harbor. Acadia also had a substantial Scots population—New Scotland—and although not far from Quebec, it was not primarily a French-speaking province as its neighbor was and is to this day. The New York Tories blended well with the English and Scots of Nova Scotia. Few returned to New York where they had been ostracized by the "patriots."

Concluding Thoughts on the War of Independence

The French military presence in America from July 1780 to November 1782 was a unique event in American history. During that time they engaged in one battle—Yorktown—which was a siege that lasted from September 30, 1781, to October 19, less than a month. The losses on all sides were minimal at Yorktown, but the victory of the American and French armies supported by the French fleet turned around a war in stalemate, and its effect caused Great Britain to give up their colony in the Western Hemisphere. The French campaign as allies with the United States accomplished the purpose for which it had been sent, no more or less, a record that few military interventions can match.

The French nation contributed three critical elements to the final result. Without all three the result would surely have been different. The first was the presence of a large naval fleet under the command of Admiral de Grasse, which controlled the ocean off Chesapeake Bay. Second was the presence of a large land army under the command of General Rochambeau, which had the experience to conduct the siege—a combat strategy unknown to Americans—that forced Cornwallis to surrender before many lives were lost. Third were the funds that the French gave the new nation, which at the time was virtually bankrupt and could not properly supply its soldiers with arms or ammunition.

There are other factors that fall under the above categories. First, leadership—some of which was negative, much positive. The notable Washington biographer James Thomas Flexner, in describing the battle of Yorktown, used the description "the largely French-engineered victory at Yorktown" and later "They [the British] came to realize the utter hopelessness of conquering a people who had become united against them. Washington's role in fostering this unity had been great."[55]The leadership of both Washington and Rochambeau, who did not get along that well or trust each other entirely, was outstanding when it counted. Washington gave special recognition and praise to the French engineer Major General Duportail, declaring that "his plan and conduct of the late attacks in the successful siege of Yorktown afford brilliant proofs of his military genius, and set the seal of his reputation."[56]Since he had arrived in 1777 to take over command of the engineers in the American army, there was never a poor fortification, as there had been in 1776 at the battles of Long Island and at Washington Heights. Duportail returned to France in 1783 and in 1790 was named Secretary of State for War during the French Revolution. Because of political charges against him he left for America in 1792 and bought a farm near Valley Forge in Pennsylvania for his new home. In 1801, the Emperor Napoleon I called him back to France and gave him full amnesty on all charges. He died at sea on his way back to his home in Pennsylvania.

The leadership of British Generals Clinton and Cornwallis, who followed Howe, and Admirals Arbuthnot, Graves, and Hood, was below the norm. Admiral George Rodney, their best, was at home in ill health at critical times. Top strategic leadership by Lord Germain at Whitehall was lacking because of the difficulties of communicating over three thousand miles of ocean in slow sailing ships. Generals and admirals were entirely on their own in the eighteenth century and often did not know what the other was doing in time to make a difference. Clinton and Cornwallis came to detest each other and blamed each other for the loss of an army of seven thousand men at Yorktown. However, the biggest blunderer surely was King George III. Historian Ketchum summarizes:

> The king—a not very intelligent man who had no military experience whatever—was an obsessive meddler, and was to blame for much that went wrong. Rigid, moralistic, quick-tempered, he never forgot a grudge and insisted that on every major decision he had the final word and intended to keep it that way, no matter what. Thanks in large measure to His Royal Majesty, the deck was heavily stacked against the British.[57]

Special mention must be made for the man, not a soldier at all, that should get more credit than he usually does for the successful ending of the conflict we call the Revolutionary War. That man, of course, was Benjamin Franklin, who at age seventy-four in 1780 persuaded the French to become an ally of his country, to send their fleet to help, and to negotiate a peace treaty with Great Britain that the French had some difficulty with but finally accepted. Next to George Washington himself, no one deserves more credit than Franklin. And perhaps more remarkable, but also tragic for him, was that his son William was a British Tory, the last governor of their colony in New Jersey.

PART III

Vermont and the Richelieu River

1783–1805

Congress's Own Regiment—Disbanded

On November 15, 1783, the final year of the war, Hazen's Regiment was officially disbanded. Much of it had been furloughed in June; three hundred soldiers were discharged on June 9, including the Chartier brothers at New Windsor, Washington's encampment on the Hudson River. Many, however, refused to leave until they received their pay, which Congress was delinquent in approving. The Canadians in the regiment, such as Pierre and Jean, were unable to return to Canada. Because they had fought against them at Yorktown, the British in Canada would not allow them back. Many settled in the camps in Albany and Fishkill, where they survived on small handouts from Congress.

General Hazen was aware of their predicament. Since it was created by Congress, the regiment got few benefits and little pay—intermittent at best. The general appealed to Congress to give them land grants, but his efforts failed. However, the State of New York (which claimed half of Vermont as its land) created the Canadian and Nova Scotia Refugee Tract of 131,500 acres in northeastern New York. In 1786, some refugees were able to move there. The Chartier brothers received no pay and no pension for their service. Years later (1837), their spouses would appeal for help when they were in strained circumstances.

The same would happen to General Hazen. In 1786, at the age fifty-three, he had a stroke that disabled him for life. All his land along the Richelieu River was declared forfeited by the privy council in London and was taken by the Governor General of Canada. Hazen died in 1803 in Troy, New York. His widow spent years, until her death in 1827, trying to recover money from the Congress and the States of New York and Vermont. Only after her death did Congress award anything to benefit Hazen's nephews and nieces.

The Chartier Brothers: Marriage and Return to Lake Champlain

By the time the Chartier brothers had been honorably discharged from the regiment in June 1783 they had both married. The older, Pierre, had married Polly, the daughter of James Robinson (Robinett in French), a sergeant major in Hazen's Regiment who died at Crown Point on the retreat out of Canada in

1776, having brought his family with him. Pierre and Polly would have a family of six children, the first of which was Peter Jr., born in West Point, New York, "where we were then stationed on the 5th day of July, 1778, and the other James was born at Fishkill, New York, on the 13th day of May A.D. 1781." The other four children were: Jacob, Joseph, Sally, and Fanny. A soldier in Captain Olivier's company, who served with Pierre, declared that "he was present in the spring of 1780 when Peter Chartier and Polly Robinson agreed to live together as man and wife until they should be able to find some Roman Catholic priest to solemnize this marriage that occurred at or near Fishkill; that subsequently in the spring of 1782 about three miles from the barracks at Fishkill he was present when the marriage of Peter and Polly was solemnized by a Roman Catholic priest who came from Philadelphia to visit the Roman Catholics of the Regiment. Polly was in her nineteenth year of age at the time and is now in her 74th year of age dated May 1837."[58]

Jean Chartier, eighteen months younger than Pierre, waited until just before his discharge to marry Sally Robinson (Robinett), Polly's sister. They had found a Catholic priest in Fishkill, Father Francis Valley, to perform the rite on May 13, 1783. Polly was present, standing as a witness for her sister. Following his discharge, the couple went to Ticonderoga on Lake Champlain for a number of years. Their son Alexander and two daughters, one of whom died as an infant, were born there. Jean was employed by Alexander Pemak. Subsequently they moved north on the lake to the town of Vergennes, Vermont, where Jean found work in the sawmill built by General Strong (more on this will follow). In 1837, Mercy Strong, widow of General John Strong's son Samuel, said that she had known Jean and Sally Chartier as tenants of her late husband. Later in life they moved from Vergennes to Massena, New York, near the St. Lawrence River and west of the Adirondack Mountains where their son Alexander lived. Jean died there in 1832. After his death, Sally stated, "The following are my reasons for removing from the State of Vermont. The only son on whom I mainly depend for support in the decline of life and with whom I do now and have ever lived removed to this state [New York] and [I] intend to remain here. Sally Chartier, Massena, New York 1839."

The correspondence quoted above about the Chartier brothers and their wives, the Robinson or Robinett sisters, were statements they had made to official recorders, as they were not literate and signed their names with an x mark. Their purpose, in 1837, was to obtain some of the pension money owed their husbands from the federal and state governments for their service to the country in Hazen's Regiment.* They, like most other soldiers in that regiment, had received nothing but the offer of some land from New York State. They lived hand to mouth, mostly in Vergennes, Vermont, employed by both Generals Strong, father and son. They were illiterate and uneducated, with no schooling available in French Canada except at monasteries and nunneries. To be a tenant farmer or forester was the occupation of most men in the Lake Champlain area. But for a professional like Jean François Arnoux—a surgeon—there were other options.

John Strong of Vergennes, Vermont

Although there had been French settlements along the shores of Lake Champlain since 1609 when Samuel de Champlain had discovered it for New France, they were temporary for fur trading and usually abandoned. It was not until the eighteenth century that a few French Canadians such as Jean Chartier took a proprietary interest in the land for lumbering (noted earlier). The earliest English settlement, which became permanent, was along the east bank of the lake where Otter Creek discharged its water after running seventy miles through Vermont hills (Otter Creek rises in Dorset Mountain). In 1765 or 1766, a Scotsman, Donald McIntosh, and a colonist from Connecticut, John Strong, separately decided to build homes about seven miles upstream on Otter Creek to avoid flooding should the lake rise. This was the beginning of a community that later would be called Vergennes, named after the French foreign minister who greatly helped America during the War of Independence.

At the time these two men and their wives located there, the British Government in London had just decided that the land west of the Connecticut River, which is the State of Vermont today, would be a part of their colony of New York. This began a struggle over the New Hampshire Grants, which was not settled until 1791 when Vermont became the fourteenth state to join the union.

To go back in time, when New England was settled by the Puritans in the seventeenth century, colonies were formed each with a royal governor, appointed by the Crown, and borderlines between them were agreed upon after

---

* The dates on the statements are from recollections of up to sixty years and may not be reliable.

some minor disputes. Thus Massachusetts, Connecticut, Rhode Island, and New Hampshire became colonies of Great Britain, along with New York. However, a border between New York and New Hampshire was never settled upon. There was no English population in the area between the Connecticut River and Lake Champlain, only Native tribes. New York became a royal colony in 1664 and New Hampshire followed in 1679. However it was not until 1747 that a royal governor of New Hampshire was appointed. His name was Benning Wentworth, and he acted as if it was in his authority to make grants of land west to Lake Champlain. In 1749 he granted land to enable the founding of Bennington (Vermont today; New Hampshire then). This was followed by the Seven Years' War when no grants were made, but soon thereafter, in 1764, the British government in London awarded all land west of the Connecticut River to New York. The towns of Bennington and Brattleboro were outraged, and the Green Mountain Boys led by Ethan Allen were formed to protest. Meanwhile, Governor Wentworth made many more grants in the area between the river and the lake, which became known as the "New Hampshire Grants" (Vermont today).

With the advent of the War of Independence, the dispute between the Green Mountain Boys and the Yorkers (they were called) was put in abeyance for a time, until January 1777 when, at Westminster, the leading citizens of Vermont proclaimed their land an independent state—independent of Great Britain and independent of the Continental Congress in Philadelphia as well. A state constitution was adopted and a governor elected. In Philadelphia, the Congress refused to recognize either—after much pressure from New York, which was claiming their land had been confiscated. So from 1777 to 1791 Vermont became an independent country. The feeling became so hostile for a time that Vermont leaders flirted with becoming a part of British Canada, until cooler heads prevailed after 1783. Only in 1791, eight years later, did Vermont join the Union of the United States of America with borders along the Connecticut River on the east and Lake Champlain on the west.

John Strong had been born on August 16, 1738, making him a contemporary of Ethan Allen. He was the son of Noah and Deborah Strong and the great great grandson of the John Strong who immigrated on *Mary and John* in 1630 to settle in Dorchester, Massachusetts. In 1759 he married Agnes McCure in Salisbury, Connecticut. She was the only daughter of a wealthy Scotsman who had to flee his country because of the rebellion there in 1715. In 1765, John and Agnes Strong left Salisbury to look for a home in the Vermont wilderness on the eastern side of Lake Champlain. He selected an area for a farm in Addison County, upon which he built a "rude house" or cabin. He and his family—a wife and three children, ages six, three, and one and a half—moved in February of 1766. The following June, a fourth child, said to be the first English child, was born in that county. Five more would follow. With the Seven Years' War being over, Strong could clear the land, plow the fields, and provide for his family. There were dangers, however, from bears as well as from Indians and later the British. For his first decade there he did benefit from trade with the British fortress at Crown Point across the lake by supplying produce for which "high prices were paid for everything supplied by his plantation."[59]

All this changed in June 1777 when British General John Burgoyne, coming south from Montreal, captured Crown Point before moving on to Saratoga where he was defeated by the American army under General Gates. The Strong family fled from the Redcoats and were separated in the process as the Iroquois tribes burned the countryside—including their cabin and farm buildings. A long separation and search was not ended until John finally found his family at Dorset, Vermont, where they made their home until the War of Independence was over in 1783. He represented Dorset in the state legislature from 1779 to 1782 and was a judge for the county in 1782.

With the war's end, the Strongs returned to Vergennes to start all over again. On the large farm they built a new house that five generations of Strongs would occupy.* As a large landowner John became a community leader. In May 1783 he and the other proprietors met at the local inn and voted "to sequester ten acres of land, together with the privilege of the falls on Otter Creek, for mill building, to John Strong, lying at the northeast corner of Panton [a section near Vergennes], on condition said Strong build a good saw-mill at the above mentioned place by the 20 of November 1783, and a good gristmill by the 20 of August 1784, that shall run at the times above mentioned."[60] The firm of Strong and Chipman built a gristmill on the island that they sold in February 1810. Lumbering and milling using waterpower from Otter Creek began in 1783 at Vergennes. The mill attracted workmen from French Canada, and it was around this time that Pierre Chartier, with his wife Polly and their children, came to Vergennes and found work with John Strong. He had recently

---

* The Strong house in Vergennes in 1934 was purchased by the Vermont Daughters of the American Revolution (DAR) and is today a museum open to the public.

been discharged from the army of the United States (see previous chapter). Jean and Sally came a few years later after some years spent at Ticonderoga. They lived in Panton between Vergennes and the lake.

Lumbering, fishing, and milling were not the only businesses that came to Vergennes. The Monkton Iron Company chose it as well in 1800, and with it came many new people. The population rose rapidly from only a few people in 1783 to about two hundred in 1790, mostly of English ancestry. By 1800 there were 516 according to the census, and 835 in 1810. "Between the years 1800 and 1810 about three hundred French Canadians settled in Vergennes. This influx was due to the development of the Monkton Iron Works, which had a need for labor. 'French Village' on the west side of Otter Creek came into being at that time, and three boarding houses were erected to care for their laborers who worked for ten dollars a month and their keep."[61] It appears that these French Canadians, who were not listed in the 1810 census, may have been transient workers as opposed to residents. By 1818 there were twenty Catholic families, all Canadian except for two English ones named Nash and Miller. The Canadians of "French Village" lived primarily on East Street and added color to the community. "Among them were some quaint and original characters, ever ready to give expression in broken English to their wit and drollery, or to relate the adventures of their lives in Canada, some of them in lumber camps and some of them in the Northwest or Hudson's Bay Company."[62]

The Roman Catholic presence in Vergennes began with missionary priests performing Mass and other holy rites such as marriage. The first Mass was held in 1776, the second not until 1816, conducted by a priest from Chambly in Canada, Father Pierre Marie Mignault, who was directed by his Bishop in Quebec to minister in the State of Vermont. After him, a priest from Montreal came for visits between 1815 and 1818. A proper Roman Catholic parish was not organized, however, until 1834 because of the opposition of town authorities. The site of St. Peter's Church was purchased in 1846. The building itself was built in 1874 and consecrated as L'Eglise de Saint Pierre one hundred years after the first Mass was held, a clear example of the strong prejudice against Roman Catholics by the English-speaking people in New England.

After his return to Vergennes, John Strong was elected to the state legislature as representative from Addison County in the years 1784, 1785, and 1786. In 1785 he was elected first judge of the Court of Addison, and in 1786 he became a judge of probate and a council member, holding these offices until

1801. He was also a member of the Vermont Convention that ratified the United States Constitution in 1791 upon its admission to the Union. He was a member of the Congregational Church of Addison, and it was said he was "a man of liberal ideas and ways."[63]

John Strong died in 1816 at the age of seventy-eight. Along with Ethan Allen, he was among the first Vermont statesmen. His oldest son Samuel succeeded his father as community leader and landholder at Vergennes. In September 1812, he raised a body of soldiers to relieve the garrison at Plattsburgh, New York, and gained victory over British forces in 1814, preventing their march further south to attack New York City. He became a major general of the state militia. Samuel Strong and his wife Mercy were friends and landlords of Sally and Polly Chartier and would testify on their behalf later on.

Jean François Arnoux in Canada

Great Britain and France had been at peace from the signing of the Treaty of Paris in 1763 until mid-summer 1778, only fifteen years, when Britain again declared war on its rival after France began to actively support Britain's American colonies in their struggle for independence. With this declaration the French-speaking Canadians again were torn between two imperial powers as they had been in previous wars. They were friendly with Americans and their interests, and many, such as the Chartier brothers, would fight against the British army. From 1778 to 1783 the Canadians of Quebec kept a low profile while the army of British General Burgoyne was in their country. Those who exhibited any sympathy with Americans were treated harshly.

The Chartiers who had remained in St. Antoine during this difficult period were Joseph and wife Marie Hubert, their eldest son Joseph, daughter Ursule, a younger son Jacques, and youngest daughter Cecile. Joseph, head of the family, was sixty years old. Pierre, Jean, and probably Antoine were away at war. With the peace treaty in 1783 they looked forward to seeing them again. Although not being able to reside in Canada, they may have come down the Richelieu River to St. Antoine for short visits. In 1789, Joseph Chartier died at age seventy, and his son Joseph became the head of the family. The father had lived long enough to be present at his daughter Cecile's wedding.

With the return of peace in Europe in 1783, the tension in Canada between the French speakers and their English rulers began a slow decline but would never disappear entirely. The French, mostly Roman Catholics, were in a great majority in the Province of Quebec and its cities Montreal and Quebec. The immigrants of English ancestry began to settle more to the west in Ontario, the city of Toronto, and other western provinces. This tension was also felt in the State of Vermont where French speakers held almost no political positions and the Roman Catholic faith was barely tolerated, as has been noted. It was into this environment that the surgeon Jean François Arnoux moved after the battle at Yorktown.

Nothing is known of his whereabouts after the surrender of Cornwallis in October 1781. Having been wounded in the knee, it is likely that he remained in and around Williamsburg, Virginia. He could have been receiving pay then and certainly received care and sustenance from his countrymen. He could have remained with them all the way back to Boston, Massachusetts, where they boarded ships for the Caribbean. Somewhere along this path, however, he must have departed from the security of his countrymen and headed north into a world of English-speaking Americans, knowing little if any of their language. What he had learned from the Chartier brothers in Yorktown about their family back in Canada, and what he may have known about his father's relation, the surgeon-major André Arnoux, was drawing him toward Montreal. He may have tried to locate the brothers in Ticonderoga or in Vergennes, where they were by 1783, and may even have worked in Vergennes as a doctor. In any event he was rapidly learning the English language, albeit with a heavy French accent.

When Jean François Arnoux first entered Canada about 1785, he must have tried to find the Chartier family living in St. Antoine. Their daughter Cecile was only fifteen years old then, not yet of marriageable age. So the surgeon must have practiced his profession somewhere in the Montreal area waiting for the time that Joseph and Marie would give their consent to the marriage of their youngest child. In 1787, on May 20 when the bride was seventeen and the groom was thirty-five, the marriage did occur, but not at St. Antoine. The couple was wed at the small village of L'Acadie about thirty miles up the Richelieu River from her family homestead and that much closer to the United States-Canadian border. L'Acadie was near the larger town of St. Jean where General Moses Hazen's lands were located near the United States border. Here they would remain while three of their children were born, only a few miles from safety.

There were good reasons why they wanted to live nearer the border than at St. Antoine, in addition to having a home of their own. Because the British authorities in Montreal knew the "French" doctor had fought against them at Yorktown, they were suspicious and watched him carefully. And when the British and French went to war against each other again in 1793, the Arnoux family must have felt vulnerable, even though there was no fighting in Canada or the United States at that time.

Jean François and Cecile Arnoux's first child, born on October 9, 1788, was a boy named Antoine—Anthony in English—after the Chartier homestead. The second, born circa 1790, was Jean François, named after his father; and the third was a girl, born on June 8, 1791, and named Cecile after her mother. They were all baptized in L'Acadie.[64] It is not certain when they departed from Canada. It may have been as early as 1792, but more likely was in 1794 after the British-French war had started. Cecile lost a child at birth in 1793, and the others were born later in Vergennes. Family history, which could have been exaggerated, tells that, "The British set a price on his head [Arnoux's] for his part in the rebellion of the colonies. They sewed gold coins in their stays and clothing and made their way to Vergennes in the State of Vermont."[65]

Another European War

During the last years of the Arnoux family's stay in L'Acadie, Quebec, the French Revolution began in Europe. King Louis XVI, desperately short of funds needed to avoid national bankruptcy, had no choice but to call out the Estates-General, France's long-dormant representative body, to meet at Versailles in May 1789. The Third Estate, the commoners, determined for a change, formed a National Assembly to write a new constitution for France, whereupon the king declared all meetings null and void and dissolved both bodies. The result was the storming of the Bastille on July 14, with a new National Assembly forming a government for France without an aristocracy and with a very limited monarchy. The king and queen were forced to leave Versailles and move to the Tuileries in Paris where they remained as prisoners for two years. In June 1791 they attempted to escape from Paris to Austrian territory but were captured before leaving the country, arrested and confined in the Conciergerie. France was then governed by the Paris Commune, led by Danton, Marat, and Robespierre. On January 21, 1793, Louis XVI was executed on the guillotine, followed by his queen Marie Antoinette eight months later, and on February 1, France declared war on Great Britain, Holland, and Spain, soon joined by Austria and Prussia. As far as the French Canadians were concerned, Britain and France were at war again after only ten years of peace, and their loyalties were again being tested.

Out of the chaos of the French Revolution, Napoleon I came to power in 1799 as First Consul and head of an army that proceeded to win victories throughout Europe until finally losing to the British at sea at Trafalgar in 1805 and to the British and Prussians on land at Waterloo in 1815. With the Peace Treaty signed at the Congress of Vienna that year, more than twenty years of turmoil had ended.

The Arnouxs in Vergennes

Vergennes in the 1790s when the Arnoux family came to live there was a farming area but also had both a sawmill and a gristmill that had been built by John Strong (see earlier pages). Lumbering along Otter Creek was an industry of consequence then, and there was a need for more labor. Enough people were in residence for the services of a doctor. Arnoux could have had patients and was most likely the only trained medical person in the area. Otter Creek provided waterpower for milling and the community grew. Soon the Monkton Iron Works was established, and with it came more French-speaking Canadians to make the Arnouxs feel that they were back at L'Acadie. More people began to come north from southern Vermont, also attracted by excellent farming land along Lake Champlain and the beginning of a dairy industry. Perhaps some thought it was strange that Vergennes had the name of a Frenchman who helped achieve their independence from Britain and died in 1787.

The town leader and largest landholder was John Strong. Another was Peter Ferris, who built a home nearer the big lake, which was given the name Ferrisburg and became the site of ship building in the nineteenth century.

The Arnoux family had friends—certainly the families of Pierre and Jean Chartier, who lived there much longer than they did. The Arnouxs had more children while in Vergennes, probably three more boys: Edward, Arthur, and the last, Gabriel, who was born on January 19, 1805. Six children, five boys and one girl, from Anthony age seventeen to newborn Gabriel, was not an uncommonly large family, but much hard work was required to support them.

Sadly, later that year their father, Jean François, died at the age of fifty-three and was buried in Vergennes. His wound at Yorktown had taken its toll, and the need to support a wife and family of six must have placed a strain on his health. It was apparent to Cecile that without a husband she and her children would have to move to where her sons could learn a craft or trade to support the family; that could only be done through apprenticeship in that era. Fortunately, her two older sons at seventeen and sixteen years were eager and able to learn a skill, but it would not be in Vermont.

PART IV

Two Families Come Together

19TH AND 20TH CENTURIES

The Arnoux Family in New York City after 1805

Shortly after the death of her husband, Cecile Chartier Arnoux made the decision to leave Vermont for New York City, a large change to be sure, but at least the family had lived in Vergennes long enough to have become completely conversant in the English language. The city also had its attractions: the opportunity for work for all who were willing to learn a craft or trade, and a rapidly expanding population promising more work in the future.

During the 1790s, New York City's population had continued to soar, passing its rival Philadelphia to become the largest city in the country. This growth continued in the following decade, so that by 1810 the census showed that there were 96,370 New Yorkers, an almost two-hundred-percent increase in twenty years. Emigration from Ireland was largely responsible for this extraordinary growth. DeWitt Clinton had been appointed Mayor in 1803, beginning a long tour of duty that lasted until 1815. He was considered one of the very best city leaders.

This period of steady prosperity was twice interrupted, once when President Jefferson's Embargo of 1807 to 1809 placed a total ban on all vessels leaving U.S. ports to protect American seamen being impressed onto British and French ships. The Embargo Act turned out to be a colossal blunder and brought an almost complete halt to trade in New York and other U.S. cities. Jefferson did not seek a third term, and Congress immediately rescinded the law after he left office. Prosperity resumed for two years until the United States declared war on Great Britain on June 18, 1812—another blunder—and again free trading was interrupted for the two years this struggle lasted. From its ending in 1815 to 1835 there was a prolonged period of revival and growth for the country and the city. The population of the city went from 100,000 in 1815 to 270,000 in 1835. It was into this community that the Arnoux family moved.

The first reference to them in the New York City Directories (similar to telephone books of today) was John Arnoux, mason, in 1810 at 62 Mulberry Street. The next year and for several thereafter his address was on Reade Street, north of City Hall. Probably Cecile and all her family lived there as well. John, the second son, had found work as a mason or bricklayer, a craft that was in great demand. Anthony, her eldest son, was listed first in 1813 as a tailor, also on Reade Street, nearby with a separate number. In the following year he moved to 46 Fair Street, which soon became Fulton Street (1816) with the establishment of the Fulton Market. This was an excellent location for a merchant tailor shop—near a market center and the dock for ferries from Brooklyn. Anthony, joined later by his youngest brother Gabriel, would remain on Fulton Street for many years, building a prosperous business as members of the New York Chapter of the "Merchant Taylor's Guild."

Before he reached this status in the Guild, Anthony had gone to London to apprentice, probably soon after the family had arrived in New York and after John had found work as a mason. From 1810 to 1812 would have been a likely time.[66] He would have been in his early twenties. In London he would have gone to the Merchant Taylor's Guild Hall at 30 Threadneedle Street, where it had been located since 1345, and there been assigned an apprenticeship. The purpose of the guilds was to regulate trade and commerce. Their function was monopolistic: to control who could trade in a commodity or enter a craft. Entry was governed by strict rules of apprenticeship that required passage of a final test on competency before becoming a master of the craft and starting a business. In New York City as in London, there were guilds for all trades and crafts, which in the latter were an offshoot of the Livery Companies. For someone such as Anthony Arnoux, a London apprenticeship for a year or two would ensure the Guild's approval and the opportunity to open a shop in New York. Without it he would have been blacklisted. The Merchants Taylor's Guild in New York controlled the number of tailors permitted to operate shops. Since the cloth they used came mostly from England, without that seal of approval the tailor would have nothing to sell.

A few blocks north of Arnoux's tailor's shop was another tailor who had been in the business since 1794. His place of business was located on Water Street, also near the Fulton Market. His name was Jonas Mapes. A generation older than Arnoux, Mapes was not only a master tailor but also an alderman of the Common Council, the city's governing body, and in 1814 a Brigadier General in the state militia preparing to defend his city against an invasion by the British navy. Fortunately that never happened. Certainly Arnoux knew him personally from the Tailor's Guild meetings. Anthony and later Gabriel Arnoux were friendly competitors with Jonas Mapes and his son-in-law, Victor B. Waldron. There was enough business for many tailors. In expanding New York, they were the only source for clothing before the large department stores opened.

The first of Cecile Arnoux's children to marry was her nineteen-year-old daughter, Mary, who wed Conway Armstrong on April 21, 1810, at Christ Church in New York. Her son Anthony followed marrying Gertrude Freeland after his return from London. Mary's marriage to Armstrong, however, was dissolved following the disclosure that he was still married to Barbara, his lawful wife at the time of his wedding to Mary. The annulment was accompanied by a public confession in 1815 witnessed by the minister of the church, Mary's brother Anthony and his wife Gertrude together with two others. (See Appendix D.) A year later Mary would marry a French immigrant who was twenty years older than she was. His name was Jean Baptiste Aiguier, a confectioner of Warren Street in the city.

Jean Baptiste Aiguier, c. 1769–1851

The area forty miles north of the city of Marseille is called "Les Monts de Vaucluse"—the Vaucluse Mountains—of Provence. These are not high mountains like the Alps, but more like large hills, the highest of which is 1,000 to 1,200 meters. The Aiguies River flows from these hills into the Rhone River at the town of Orange, north of Avignon. Left over when the Ice Age receded to the north, the Vaucluse hills have a rocky soil that is ideal for the growth of vineyards producing the famous Château Neuf-du-Pape wine. Another geological feature left by the glacier is a reserve of rainwater in the rocks fed by small ditches cut through them by nature. The French call these special features "aiguiers." A section of the Vaucluse plateau in the Luberon Valley near the town of Rustrel is an area called "Le Pays des Aiguiers"—the country of Aiguiers—because of the large concentration of them—more than ten. They are so named on a trail map for walkers. Also in "Le Pays des Aiguiers" is Mount St. Pierre, at 1255 meters, and the small villages of Rustrel, Lagarde, Villars, Saignon, Saint-Christol, and the larger town of Apt. Not too far away is the ancient capital of Provence, Aix, where the painter Cezanne was born and painted for much of his life.

In the early nineteenth century where Cezanne would later paint Mont St. Victoire in the Vaucluse and many other landscapes, French families were working the vineyards in Le Pays des Aiguiers. The son of one of these decided that he wanted a new life for himself. He went to Marseille and boarded a ship for New York. We don't know the name of the ship, but most likely he left before the start of the War of 1812 between Great Britain and the United States. When he arrived in New York he identified himself as Jean Baptiste Aiguier.

Why would a Frenchman, twenty-five to thirty years old, come to New

F. et C. MORENAS

LE PAYS
DES AIGUIERS

AU CŒUR DES MONTS DE VAUCLUSE
CE "LUBERON D'EN FACE"

Auberge de Jeunesse Regain
SAIGNON (Vaucluse)

The official guide of the countryside in the Vaucluse mountains of Provence.

Les Aiguiers de Villars

A typical aiguier in Villars.

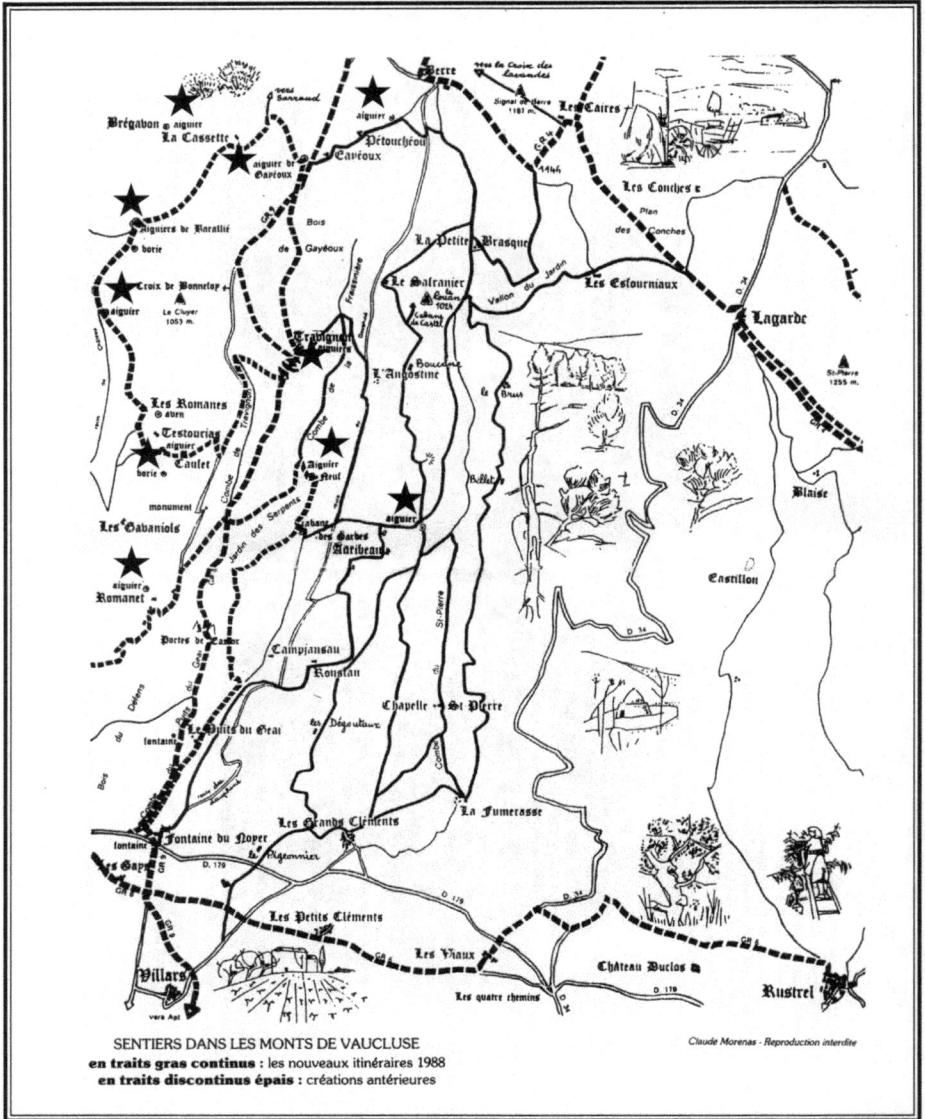

SENTIERS DANS LES MONTS DE VAUCLUSE
en traits gras continus : les nouveaux itinéraires 1988
en traits discontinus épais : créations antérieures

Claude Morenas · Reproduction interdite

A 1988 map of footpaths between Villars and Berre includes ten different aiguiers, marked with stars, in the Vaucluse mountains.

York? Almost no French were immigrating to America that early, when Napoleon was Emperor of France and conqueror of much of Europe. Could Jean Baptiste have known of the Arnoux family of Marseille, one of whom was a doctor and ship's surgeon? It is possible—but not likely—that he knew the Arnoux family that arrived in New York from Vergennes, Vermont, in 1805. The answer is not known.

In any event, Jean Baptiste Aiguier and Mary Cecilia Arnoux were married in October 1816 in the parsonage of the First Moravian Church of New York City at 44 Fair Street (soon to be changed to Fulton Street) by the Reverend B. Mortimer in the presence of the bride's brother and sister-in-law, Anthony and Gertrude Arnoux. It should be noted that although both husband and wife had been brought up in communities in Provence and French-speaking Canada that were strongly Roman Catholic, they chose to be married by a Moravian minister in his parsonage. The Moravians were a small Christian sect in New York that came from Protestants in sixteenth-century Czech Moravia. Their first church building in Manhattan opened on Fair Street in 1751, later moving uptown in 1869. The large Moravian Cemetery is situated in Staten Island, where many of the Demarest family were buried. (See page 146.)

From the union of Jean Baptiste Aiguier and Mary Cecilia Arnoux a daughter and two sons were born. Emily Frances was born c. 1818, married Thomas Kennett, Gabriel Arnoux's brother-in-law, in 1837 and lived thereafter in Buffalo, New York. She was given the middle name of her maternal grandfather, Jean François Arnoux. The second child was Jean Baptiste (Jr.) born in 1821. He was usually called John B. Aiguier. He had seven children with his first wife, Lucy Doe. After her death in 1877, he married Josephine (surname unknown), from which there was no issue. He became a jeweler by trade and lived at 145 Reade Street. John died in 1890. The youngest child was named Gabriel after his uncle Gabriel Arnoux. He was born in 1828. More about him will follow.

The family of Jean Baptiste and Mary Cecilia Aiguier lived in a house that he had purchased sometime after 1829 at 44 Thomas Street, north of Duane Street and west of what is today Court House Square in Manhattan. As an alien resident (late of France) Jean Baptiste had to file with New York State in order to own property. This he did on April 29, 1829. In the New York Directory he is described sometimes as "a cook" and also as "a confectioner" of sweets, candies, or fancy desserts.

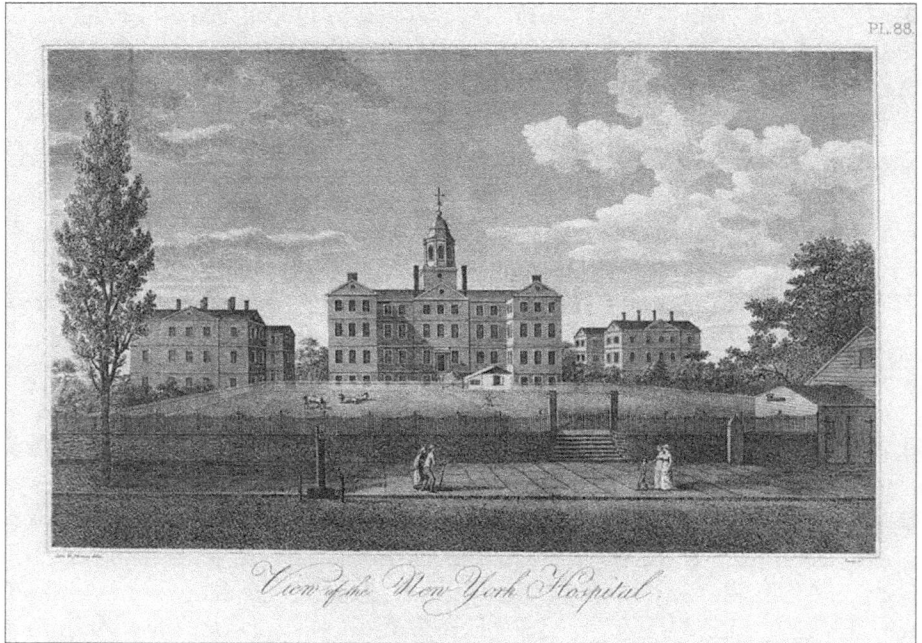

The view from Broadway between Duane and Worth Streets in 1811. The hospital was near 44 Thomas Street, home of J. B. Aiguier and family after 1829.

FULTON ST. & MARKET.

The Moravian Church where Jean Baptiste Aiguier and Mary Cecile Arnoux were married in 1816 was up the street on the left near the tailor shop of Anthony and Gabriel Arnoux. Anthony was a witness at the wedding.

Anthony and Gabriel Arnoux: New York Tailors, 1820–1850

The last of Cecile Arnoux's children to marry was Gabriel, who as an infant came to New York from Vergennes and never knew his father. Gabriel had joined his older brother Anthony in the merchant tailor firm of Anthony and Gabriel A. Arnoux in 1824–1825. A year later he married Ann Kennett from Norwalk, Connecticut. There were several children from his marriage.

With the completion of the Erie Canal in 1825, New York was assured of its status as the largest city in the nation as well as the largest port. There were interruptions to its growth such as the yellow fever outbreak in the summer of 1822, when upwards of fifty thousand people fled the city, followed by epidemics of cholera, typhus, and typhoid fever, which came from ships from Europe throughout the nineteenth century. There were also the two great fires of 1835 and 1845 that destroyed large segments of the city but resulted in rebuilding where old seventeenth-century structures had stood. The other major interruption to the city's growth was the financial panic of 1837 followed by several years of depression.

On the positive side, however, was an increase in Irish and German immigration, the coming of the railroads, and the advent of steam-powered ships. In April 1838 the paddle wheel steam packet *Great Western* arrived in New York harbor only fourteen days out of Bristol in England, a record at that time.

The merchant tailor firm of Anthony and Gabriel A. Arnoux on Fulton Street had prospered from its beginning until 1836 when a strike by journeymen tailors threatened that business in New York. Three years earlier, during a period of sharp inflation in the cost of food, fuel, and rent, and with real wages declining, the trade journeymen in the city organized the General Trades Union of New York City (GTU) to protect their jobs. One of these was the journeymen tailors of the city. The masters of these trades, such as the Society of Master Tailors, immediately tried to crush the unions but were generally unsuccessful in their efforts. They had the law on their side in that era, but an irreparable breach had been opened up. GTU-backed strikes mounted between 1833 and 1835. The union was successful in achieving certain benefits—a ten-hour day (it had been a twelve-hour day) and the abolition of prison labor, which undercut the market. The masters were successful in breaking strikes by calling on the military to disperse protestors.

The GTU got stronger, however, and by 1836, two-thirds of New York's workingmen were enrolled in fifty-two confederated unions. The crisis came to its head that year. The Society of Master Tailors announced a wage cut for employees and said they would not employ union men. The journeymen tailors responded with a citywide strike that was supported by the GTU and other trades. Battles broke out among strikers, strike breakers, and the police. The *New York Herald* reported "a general movement over the city."

The Master Tailors turned to the courts and in late March won a conspiracy indictment against twenty striking tailors, the judge declaring that "a man has the right to work as he pleases." With this indictment the unions took to the streets, marching up Broadway with bands and banners proclaiming the right to regulate their wages. "Are we not on the eve of another revolution," the *New York Herald* said, "such as we witnessed among the mechanics in 1829?"[67]

The trial began in May 1836 with twenty tailors in the dock and lasted a month. On June 6 the judge delivered a sentence of heavy fines totaling 1,400 dollars. He added, "Labor unions are a foreign idea, mainly upheld by foreigners."[68] They had been found guilty of going on strike. A giant rally was planned in City Hall Park for the following Saturday, during which an effigy of the judge was burned. Cooler heads prevailed however, and the group resolved to form a separate party for the laboring classes. Tammany Hall was quick to pick up this mantle, giving political voice and vote to the grievances of the poor.

From the 1830s to 1850s, the garment trade began to change in New York City. Firms such as Anthony and Gabriel A. Arnoux and Mapes and Waldron, the merchant tailors, suffered a decline in business. Some custom tailors such as Brooks Brothers turned into wholesalers. An immigrant tailor might get a contract from the wholesaler, do his own cutting at home and pass the work on to sewers, bypassing the merchant tailor entirely. Then in 1846, on the east side of Broadway at Chambers Street, a very large new store opened—a new invention where clothes could be purchased ready to wear. "The Marble Palace" of Alexander T. Stewart, the pioneer department store in the country, would change the garment trade forever. It would sell clothes and tailor them, if needed, as well. Four years later Isaac Merritt Singer came to New York to build and sell his practical sewing machine. The mass production of garments was underway.

Mapes and Waldron, merchant tailors of the Guild, closed for good in 1848. The Arnoux brothers moved north from Fulton Street to a new location

Hudson River

Prince Street

Broadway

Lower Manhattan

Leonard Street

Thomas Street

Reade Street

Home of Jean Baptiste and
Mary Cecilia Aiguier

Warren Street

City Hall

Park Row — Tribune Building

Fulton Street

Broadway

Nassau Street

William Street

Arnoux Brothers–Tailors

First Moravian Church

Wall Street

East River

Map of Lower Manhattan in the mid-nineteenth century.

in the basement of the Metropolitan Hotel at Broadway and Prince Street in 1850. That being the site of the famous Niblio's Garden would have given the tailors some clients that still wanted fitted clothes. But the future was with A.T. Stewart, Brooks Brothers, Lord and Taylor, and W. J. Sloane. By then ninety-five percent of New York's tailors were born abroad, fifty-five percent were German, and thirty-four percent were Irish. The work was done at home aided by family. The customer was the wholesaler.

The Two Families at Mid-Century

On January 1, 1840, at the Thomas Street home of her daughter and son-in-law Mary Cecilia and Jean Baptiste Aiguier, Cecile Chartier Arnoux died at the age of seventy. She had been born in St. Antoine in Canada and grew up there speaking French. A Roman Catholic by faith, she married Jean François Arnoux, veteran of the battle of Yorktown and surgeon on a French warship. She and her husband had seven children, moved to Vermont, and then, as a widow, she moved the family to New York City when her offspring were all under eighteen years old. For thirty years until her death she had lived in the care of her family, mostly with her daughter.

The Aiguier family lived in their house at 44 Thomas Street for the rest of their lives, well after many New York residents had moved uptown. On May 30, 1850, Mary C. Aiguier died at the age of fifty-nine. She was the first of her older siblings who had been born in L'Acadie to pass on. The following year, on September 29, her husband died as well. He was eighty-two. They were both buried at Green-Wood Cemetery in Brooklyn, beginning a long line of Aiguiers and Arnouxs who would be buried there. A monument marks the graves of the Aiguiers. Mary C. Aiguier's gravestone reads, "A Constant Christian"; Jean Baptiste Aiguier's reads, "His Hope was in Christ." (See Appendix B.)

Gabriel Aiguier

The third child and youngest son of Jean Baptiste and Mary Cecilia Aiguier was Gabriel Aiguier. On July 8, 1849, at the age of twenty-one, he married Mary Eliza Decker, the daughter of Matthew and Eliza Decker. The Decker's immigrant ancestor, Johannes De Decker, had settled in Staten Island in 1665.

Thereafter, the family became large landholders there. Gabriel and Mary Eliza had two sons: James Kurley, born in 1850, and John Matthew, after which Mary Eliza died unexpectedly in October 1855. Gabriel then married Joanna Cochran and they had four more children: Lizzie Minor, Eleanor Cochran, Gabriel Jr., and Margaret.

Gabriel became a career New York City police officer. He joined the force during the mayoralty of Fernando Wood between 1854 and 1859. In 1857 he was listed as living at 49 Leonard Street. A professional police department was very new at that time. Inspired by the example set in London, New York became the first American city to adopt a law in 1845 requiring a police force that would effectively prevent a crime as well as respond to it. Signed by then Mayor William F. Havemeyer, the law provided for up to eight hundred men who were identified by a star-shaped badge. Uniforms for the force were adopted in 1850. It was a very small force, only 1,200 officers in 1855, for a city with 600,000 people. At the time of the draft riot in 1863 there were only 2,500 police officers available to keep the peace and ensure the safety of such a large population.

In 1857, when Gabriel Aiguier was a very junior officer, the state legislature, dominated by the Republicans, decided to establish a Metropolitan Police District composed of New York, Kings (Brooklyn), Westchester (Bronx), and Richmond (Staten Island)—all separate cities before 1898. New York's Mayor Fernando Wood, a Democrat, resisted the establishment of a state force within the city and vowed to continue his own police force. The two coexisted for thirteen years until 1870 when the Democratic-controlled state legislature abolished the Metropolitans, as they were called, and returned control to the mayor's local police force. The worst conflict that occurred during the years with two police forces was in June of 1857, when the Metropolitans sought to arrest Mayor Wood for inciting a riot and a battle ensued on Broadway. Blood was shed and several officers on both sides were injured. The State Court of Appeals upheld the constitutionality of the state police, which quieted the scene, but the fact that there was a divided police presence in New York during the Civil War made the force almost ineffective during the much greater crisis in July 1863.

The draft riots (as they were later called) from July 13 to 16, 1863, were the bloodiest urban disturbances in American history and remain so today. Ironically, the background does not begin with the draft at all, but with President

Gabriel Aiguier, 1886, age 58, nearing retirement.

Lincoln's Emancipation Proclamation that was promulgated on January 1 that year, though it freed no slaves outside the southern states. The opposition to the emancipation of slaves by former Mayor Fernando Wood and New York's Peace Democrats, who wanted to end the killing and return to the status quo, inflamed the majority of Irish Democrats who were fearful that they would lose their jobs to the freed slaves from the south. Wood and his followers delivered several orations—which were anti-Lincoln, antiwar, and anti-black—that brought the Irish to a fever pitch. Antiwar activism reached a high point on June 3, 1863, when Wood held a massive Peace Convention at Cooper Union at which orators declared the war was a rich man's fight, undermining the Constitution, and would flood New York with southern blacks. Following this convention three thousand Irish longshoremen went on strike, refusing to load army transports. As cotton bales began to accumulate on piers, the railroad hired blacks as strikebreakers only to have one thousand white strikers drive them away.

This was the environment in New York City, while in Pennsylvania, near Harrisburg, General Robert E. Lee's Army of Northern Virginia crossed the Potomac River on June 29 to take a position near the small town called Gettysburg. Should he defeat General Meade's army opposing him there, the way to New York would be wide open and Wood and the Peace Democrats would have their way. Thousands of troops were sent from New York to join Meade's army, and by July 1 New York was stripped of its defenses. There were only 550 men in eight forts and no military vessels in New York Harbor. To maintain order there were only 2,500 police officers under two separate commands.

Back in March, due to heavy Union losses and soaring desertion rates, Congress had passed the National Conscription Act requiring all men aged twenty to thirty-five (and all unmarried men thirty-five to forty-five) to enroll. A lottery would then be held to choose draftees from the pool. Finally, and this was the straw that broke the camel's back, the law provided that draftees could provide a substitute to fight in their place or pay three hundred dollars—prohibitively high for working-class people—for the government to use as a recruiting bounty. The enrollment proceeded peacefully in May and June, but the lottery was postponed until July 11. The police were posted throughout the city but there was nowhere near enough, as a variety of protests were scheduled for July 13, a Monday workday.

No one went to work that morning. Hundreds of workers from all over the city began to march on the west side to Central Park and then spread out to the east side and throughout the city, causing destruction wherever they could. They had targets: Republicans in general and affluent Republicans in particular; their homes were sacked, looted, and burned. "As small detachments of police were sent to the worst areas, they were routed and stomped, their bodies stripped, their faces smashed." "Homes suspected of giving refuge to fleeing policemen were burned."[69] Telegraph poles that connected local police precincts to the central office were cut down and the lines cut. Another target was newspaper row across from City Hall Park where the *Times* and the *Tribune* had their printing offices, considered the heartland of Republicanism. The raging crowd, led by a waiter from Astor House across the Park, attacked the *Tribune* building, which had been barricaded with bales of printing paper. They stoned the building, broke in, and started a fire but were driven off by a contingent of police, one of whom was Officer Gabriel Aiguier, a junior patrolman at the time.

Then on the second and third days the target became black people. The rioters began a race war. They hunted blacks on the streets, mauled them along the docks, went after them in restaurants and hotels and in their homes around Bleecker Street. Several were hanged and burned, dragged from their houses and lynched. Civil order completely disappeared on Tuesday and throughout most of Wednesday. Most people stayed at home and prayed that the rage would pass.

Finally, on Wednesday, the worst day of violence any American city had ever seen or would see, Federal troops began to return from the victorious battle of Gettysburg and joined with volunteer companies made up of employees of merchants and barbers. Using howitzers loaded with grapeshot they mowed down rioters, and with their rifles—with bayonets attached—they entered houses and chased rioters to their deaths.

By Thursday evening it was all over. The city, filled with six thousand troops, was quiet. Telegraph lines were being repaired, rail lines that had been torn up were being replaced, the horse cars ran again, and the laborers returned to work.

There were not as many deaths as had been expected. Only 119 could be verified, mostly black men. There was little retribution, as the War Democrats were in charge of New York, not the Republicans. The latter had asked President Lincoln to declare martial law, but he had declined to take such radical

PRINTING-HOUSE SQUARE,
NEW YORK.

New York Tribune building, on left, guarded by Gabriel Aiguier during the riot in 1863. The New York Times building, in center, and troops arriving from the right.

actions. Rioters were indicted but only sixty-seven were convicted and only a handful received lengthy sentences. When the draft lottery was started up again in August, ten thousand federal troops were brought to New York to maintain the peace; they were successful. It helped when the Board of Supervisors appropriated two million dollars to buy substitutes for poor men and municipal police, firemen, and local militia. Few who did not want to serve were required to. In the short term the war boom overtook the impact of the riots and New York returned to its pre-riot condition.

Still, President Lincoln was disliked by the rank-and-file voter. In the election in November 1864, almost a year and a half later, he lost the New York City vote by 73,716 to 36,687—a decisive defeat. Of course only white males could vote, and Tammany Hall, dominated by William Tweed and his Irish henchmen, carefully watched each polling place, discouraging many from entering to cast their ballots.

Gabriel Aiguier was thirty-five years old when he and a few police colleagues were trying to protect the *Tribune* building on Park Row that terrible day. It was surely the most traumatic day in his life. As police were required to do, he was living in Manhattan, at 50 Vandam Street with his second wife Joanna and four children. Two more were born later. He had seen and experienced a time when civil disorder had taken over social discourse, and he must have realized that, as a police officer, he could do nothing about it.

For the remainder of his career as a police officer, Gabriel lived on Bleecker Street and then on Commerce Street, both on the west side in the south part of Greenwich Village. This part of the city was one of the more upscale areas that attracted successful merchants.

Gabriel retired from the police department in 1888 when he was sixty years old and moved to Brooklyn. He lived with his daughter Lizzie Aiguier Sweeney, her husband, Vaiden B. Sweeney, and their family at 245 Bainbridge Street, then a suburb of the city. When he died on December 6, 1903, he was seventy-five years old, having outlived both his wives and his two eldest sons, James Kurley and John Matthew. He was buried in Green-Wood Cemetery with the other Aiguiers.

After Gabriel's death the Sweeneys continued to live on Bainbridge Street for two decades. Their daughter Martha became engaged and married Bertram L. Aiguier, the youngest son of James Kurley Aiguier, who was Lizzie Aiguier Sweeney's older half-brother. The married couple were therefore first cousins.

Ida Amelia Demarest, Bertram Aiguier's great aunt, also came to live with them at that time.

By 1924 this extended family had moved to 3612 Farragut Road near Brooklyn College, a better neighborhood in the rapidly expanding city. Vaiden Sweeney died in 1937; Lizzie, his wife, in 1939; and Aunt Ida in 1947. Bert and Martha Aiguier, with their daughter, Joan, continued to live on Farragut Road. Bert died in 1950 and Martha in 1971.

The Deaths of Anthony and Gabriel Arnoux

Gabriel Arnoux, the youngest son in the family, died first in 1855 at the age of fifty. His wife Ann died in the same year. They were survived by a son, William Henry Arnoux, born in 1831. He became a notable judge of the New York Superior Court following a distinguished career at the New York Bar Association. Another son of Gabriel and Ann, Anthony (after his uncle), took his own life in 1884.

Anthony Arnoux (Gabriel's oldest brother), born in L'Acadie, Canada, survived him by many years. He continued in the tailoring business with the help of his nephews. He died in 1872 at the age of eighty-four at a summer home in West New Brighton on Staten Island. He and Gertrude, his wife, had lived in Brooklyn. She died in 1875. They were both buried at Green-Wood with many other Arnouxs. (See Appendix B.)

James Kurley and Lauretta Demarest Aiguier

The land on the western side of Staten Island was flat and fertile, used primarily for farming to provide food for the fast-growing population of New York City, as was the south part of Brooklyn. Both were the breadbaskets of the city. Produce from the Staten Island farms was carried from the fields in horse-drawn carts along a road called Victory Boulevard to Decker's Landing—Port Richmond today—where ferries would take it to Bayonne, New Jersey, or to markets on the west side of Manhattan along the Hudson River. Decker's Landing was so-named because the Decker family farm was the largest in western Staten Island. In 1866, following the end of the Civil War, Decker's Landing became incorporated as Port Richmond, Richmond being the county name of Staten Island. It rapidly grew in size as business through that port increased both to New Jersey and Manhattan.

Family and friends of Vaiden B. Sweeney and his wife, Lizzie Aiguier Sweeney, on Christmas night 1920 at their home on Bainbridge Street, Brooklyn. Vaiden B. Sweeney is in the center of the rear row with beard. Ida Amelia Demarest is in the center, seated at the table. Bertram L. Aiguier (her great-nephew) is seated on her right. Also in the group are Lizzie A. Sweeney, her sister, Eleanor C. Aiguier; and Vaiden and Lizzie's daughter, Martha Sweeney, who would later marry Bertram Aiguier.

After Mary Eliza Decker Aiguier's death (see page 130), her husband Gabriel had undoubtedly taken their sons James Kurley and John to Travisville to visit their Decker grandparents and perhaps to work on their farms in the summer. It became familiar to them and gave them a chance to earn money. Soon Gabriel married again and four more children were born to Joanna, his second wife. In the 1870s James Kurley had been able to establish himself as a carpenter for hire, thus adding to the family income.

It was in 1870—when James Kurley was twenty—that a new family came to Travisville to buy a small four-acre farm from the widow of Abraham Decker of the family of James's mother. The farm was in the shape of a triangle along Richmond Turnpike where it joined the Travisville Road toward New Jersey. It was about a four-mile journey north to Port Richmond. The new family was headed by Jacob J. Demarest and his wife Elizabeth Powles Demarest, who lived in Manhattan.

With their son Abraham, in 1834 the Demarests had come from Closter Dock, along the Hudson River in New Jersey, to live at several addresses in Manhattan until moving in 1855 to 364 West Eleventh Street very near the Hudson. This became their home until Jacob died in 1878. During their years in Manhattan their son Abraham met and married Sarah L. Christopher (1856) whose family came from the Castleton section of Staten Island, which was in the northeast part of the island facing New York Harbor. This connection introduced the island to the Demarest family and could have led to their purchase of the farm in 1870. Abraham and Sarah Demarest had a family of five children, the second of whom was Lauretta Elizabeth, born in December of 1858.

Following the death of Jacob Demarest in 1878, the Staten Island farm was bequeathed to his wife Elizabeth, and upon her death in 1890 to her son Abraham. Abraham and Sarah had moved there to live with their family after Jacob's death in 1878. Lauretta was twenty years old that year and would marry twenty-eight-year-old James Kurley Aiguier. In addition to being a carpenter, James had joined the New York National Guard in 1876 and had been assigned to the Second Brigade of the 71st Regiment. He was promoted to corporal and served through 1879. The regiment was in reserve status in those years, so members only had to serve two weeks a year for training.

The newly married couple set up home in Manhattan at 83 Perry Street in the West Village and then in 1881 moved to 232 West Thirteenth Street. Here their three sons were born: Percy Gabriel in 1881, James Edward in 1883, and

James K. Aiguier, circa 1875.

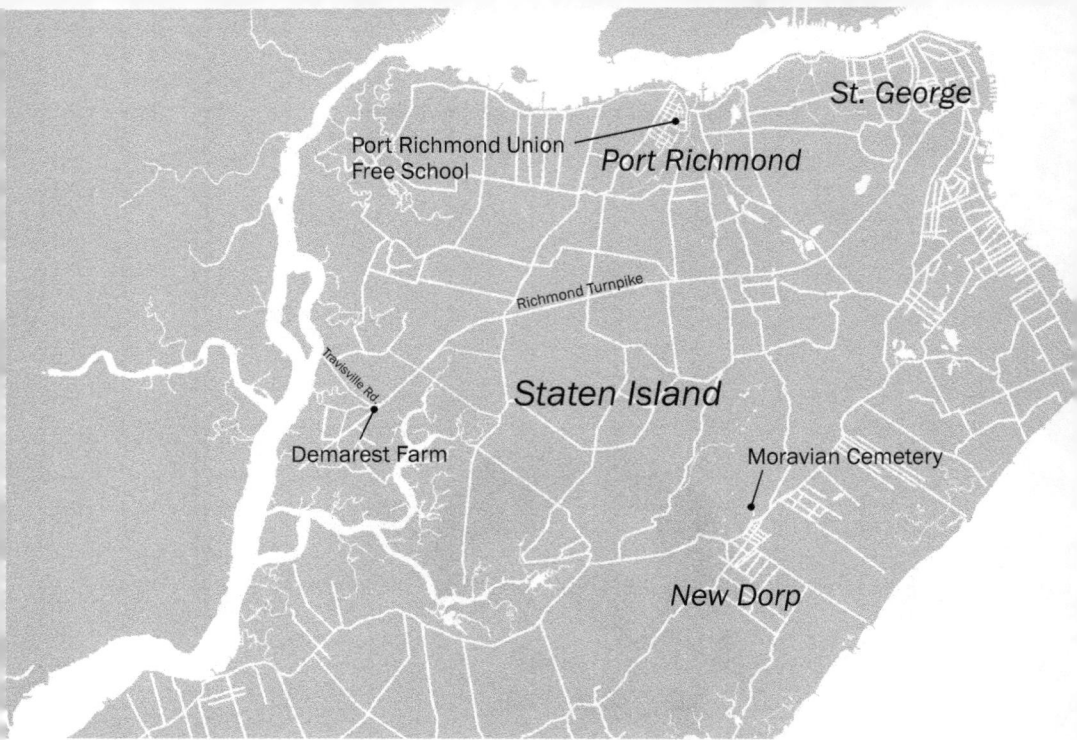

Maps of Staten Island, *above*, and Greenwich Village in Manhattan, *below*, in the late nineteenth century.

Bertram Le Roy in 1885. In time they attended the Grove Street School nearby. Much later in life, James Edward Aiguier reminisced with his daughter Eugénie Havemeyer of living there, attending the Grove Street School, visiting the West Eleventh Street house of his great grandmother Elizabeth Demarest, and playing baseball at the "farm" by the railroad tracks, which were not elevated as yet (Hudson River Railroad).

In 1892, James Kurley Aiguier died unexpectedly at the age of forty-two. Lauretta and three young boys, all under twelve, were left without support. Lauretta decided to move from Manhattan to the farm on Staten Island to live with her parents, Abraham and Sarah Demarest. In fact, it is likely that she had been considering such a move for several years because in 1887 she had purchased for $250 a plot of land twenty-five feet by 275 feet upon which there was a house that could be rented within the Port Richmond School District. Owning this would qualify her to send her sons to public school in the district.

In any event, following his father's death and his family's move to Staten Island to live on the farm, James Edward Aiguier entered the Port Richmond Union Free School (later P. S. 20) on Herberton Avenue, a distance of about four miles from the Demarest farm in Travisville. He was nine years old at the time and would go to school in the morning on the milk wagon on its trip to Port Richmond to make deliveries. It was an excellent new school. He stayed there until he was fourteen years old, receiving a first-rate education. He then left home to live with a family in Nyack along the Hudson River, where he apprenticed in their pharmacy and general store to earn money and pay his lodging. Here he completed his high school education with one year in high school and the balance at night or correspondence school.

James Edward Aiguier, 1883–1977
His Professional Education

J. E. Aiguier's professional education started when he began a two-year course of study at the College of Pharmacy of the City of New York. His time of apprenticing at the store in Nyack had appealed to him and spurred his interest in becoming a registered pharmacist. The College had existed in the city since 1831, and in 1904, while he was attending, it became a part of Columbia University in Washington Heights. Presumably he lived nearby and worked at the pharmacy of W. E. Cramer to support himself and pay his tuition. On December 28, 1904, Eddie, as he was called by family and friends, received a license from the State of New York to practice, and on April 27, 1905, he received his degree as a "Graduate" of the College of Pharmacy. This would be the first of many professional degrees he received over a distinguished career. He was then twenty-one years old.

With his Ph.G. in pharmacy, Eddie worked first at Bellevue Hospital, the large city hospital on East Twenty-Sixth Street, where he had charge of its pharmacy. This was followed by a position at the Gouverneur Hospital on the Lower East Side of New York in 1908 and 1909. Following these hospital positions he accepted employment with the drug store chain of Riker and Hegeman, one of the largest in the northeast part of the country. He would remain with Riker for four years until 1914.

The Riker chain started in 1894 with a single store in Manhattan. A second store, also in Manhattan, was opened in 1904. Over the next decade the company expanded to one hundred stores in Manhattan, Brooklyn, Boston, Philadelphia, and Washington D.C., as well as taking over the Hegeman stores. The great majority, however, were in Manhattan. In his years with Riker, Eddie worked at several of their stores, being given increasing responsibility with each change. These locations included 101st Street and Broadway; the prescription department of the store at Forty-Sixth Street and Broadway; the store at 110th Street and Broadway, where he was manager in 1912; and finally back to store number forty-nine at Forty-Sixth Street and Broadway, where he was manager of this new store in the heart of the Theater District. In October 1914 he received a company honor for the best store in the chain and was offered the post of district manager, which he declined in order to enter the University of Pennsylvania Medical School in Philadelphia. During these years he had saved money to support his mother on Staten Island. The company recognized his service in its monthly magazine *Riker Record* as follows:

James E. Aiguier

James E. Aiguier, in leaving the Riker household to enter the University of Pennsylvania, takes with him the best wishes for a successful career in the profession he has chosen for his life work, not only of his more immediate associates in Store 49, but of the host of friends he

James Edward Aiguier as a young man.

has won for himself by his courtly manners, his polished address and the sterling worth of his character.

During his management of Store 49 Mr. Aiguier built up for himself a most enviable reputation as an able executive, an efficient salesman and a capable merchandiser. Among all the Store Managers of Greater New York, Mr. Aiguier was eminent as an executive. Strong and firm in discipline, yet so kindly and suave was he in its exercise that he won both the confidence and affectionate liking of those who served under him, in a way that a more lenient and easy-going executive never can.

Under his judicious and skillful guidance, and with the splendid cooperation of Arthur Kopf and Hans Peterson, the Drug Department and Prescription room were so arranged and systematized as to be not only a model for Riker Store Managers, but as to excite the most generous commendation from entirely disinterested and competent visitors. The Poison Closet especially was regarded by those best qualified to judge as being entirely a class by itself.

Mr. Aiguier's loss will be felt, but we are entirely confident that his loss to the world of Pharmacy will be a gain to the Medical profession upon which he is about to enter.

To Mr. Aiguier we say Godspeed!

There is evidence that in 1912 Eddie applied for and received from the State of New York a medical student certificate saying that he was qualified to study for a medical degree, possibly at Columbia. However he continued with Riker for two more years and then asked that the medical student certificate be changed to a dental student certificate. By 1914, a new development at the University of Pennsylvania's Dental School had persuaded him to change his plans from medical to dental, and in October 1914 he enrolled for a degree in dental surgery at the "new" Thomas W. Evans Museum and Dental Institution, known as the Evans Institute. The "new" building, said to be the best equipped in the nation, would not open until 1915, but the faculty of the dental school was already known as "second to none." It was led by its dean, Dr. Edward C. Kirk, who was said to have persuaded Eddie (if indeed much persuasion was needed) to switch from medical to dental surgery. When he matriculated at the Evans Institute Eddie was thirty-one years old.

The University of Pennsylvania's School of Dental Medicine had been founded in 1878 and was located at several locations on the campus in the

The Riker Hegeman Drug Store on 110th Street and Broadway is shown in 1912. James E. Aiguier, Ph. G., Store Manager, is in the rear farthest to the left.

years before 1915 when the new building was completed at Fortieth and Spruce Streets. In 1897, at his death, Thomas W. Evans, confidante of Napoleon III and a brilliant, innovative dentist to the courts of Europe, had left his estate to the University of Pennsylvania for a new building at the School of Dental Medicine that would match in quality its already well-known faculty members, Dr. Matthew H. Cryer, Dr. Edwin T. Darby, and Dr. Edward C. Kirk.

Not long after Eddie started his courses at the Evans Institute, his mother Lauretta Demarest Aiguier died at home on January 1, 1915, at the age of fifty-six. She had continued to live on the farm on Staten Island with her aged parents as well as her younger brother Edward T. Demarest, whose Christian name she had given to her son. Her mother, Sarah Christopher Demarest, died on August 12, 1915, and her father, Abraham Demarest, died on January 18, 1916. All three were buried in the Staten Island Moravian Cemetery, as was her husband, James K. Aiguier (1892), and her oldest son, Percy Gabriel Aiguier (1925). Eddie had been very close to his mother and had supported her financially since he had begun working in pharmacies as a boy. She had instilled in him a sense of pride regarding his family. Her Demarest ancestors had always been of great interest to him throughout his life.

At the Evans Institute and in World War I

James Edward Aiguier matriculated at the Evans Institute in September 1914. His freshman class (Class of 1917) of 226 students was the first to use the Institute's new facilities. It was also the first class to have a married female as a student. Presiding over the School of Dental Medicine was the provost, Dr. Edgar F. Smith, and the dean, Edward C. Kirk, D. D. S. Among the most senior faculty were Edwin T. Darby, professor of operating dentistry, and Matthew H. Cryer, professor of oral surgery. All three would retire in 1917, Eddie's graduating year. A new professor in 1913 was Hermann Prinz, professor of materia medica and therapeutics, a leader in his field, who chose Eddie to be his assistant during his time at the school and who became a close professional and personal friend for many years. Both men held degrees in pharmacology, and if Eddie modeled his career after anyone, it was Dr. Prinz.

From its earliest years the School of Dental Medicine had organized honorary societies, academic in nature, honoring distinguished professors and

University of Pennsylvania School of Dental Medicine

Located at the corner of Spruce and Fortieth Streets in Philadelphia, the building honored the memory of Dr. Thomas W. Evans, who was born in that city, apprenticed there in 1841, and in 1847 moved to Paris to become well known as the dentist of Emperor Napoleon III and his queen, Eugénie. He was the first American dentist to achieve an international reputation. He died in 1897 at the age of 74.

composed of faculty and students, to promote the interests in different parts of the field of dentistry. Eligibility was governed by scholastic standing. Two early societies were: the Edwin T. Darby Dental Society, founded in 1891; and the Matthew H. Cryer Society of Oral Surgery, founded in 1912. There were a total of seven of these honorary societies. Only the top students were chosen to join them, and Eddie Aiguier joined both the Darby and the Cryer societies. In his senior year, 1916–1917, he was elected president of both. This was probably as close as one could come at that time to being the top student at the Evans Institute. No wonder he was chosen by Dr. Prinz to be his assistant. He was older, more mature, and more experienced than most of the other students, and he would find that the teaching of his profession was the aspect he most loved. Always a joiner, he was also a life member of Delta Sigma Delta, the national dental fraternity.

In April of 1917, his senior year, the United States joined the Allies, England and France, in World War I. Eddie had almost finished his three years at Evans. In March that year he was admitted to the Honorary Society of Sigma Xi, the science equivalent of Phi Beta Kappa, and on June 20, 1917, he received from the University of Pennsylvania the degree of Doctor of Dental Surgery, D.D.S. He was now Dr. Aiguier and was licensed to practice in Delaware, Pennsylvania, and New York State.

Following his graduation he joined the faculty of the Evans Institute as an assistant to Professor Prinz in the fall term of 1917–1918, but with the country at war and a draft in effect he wanted to serve his country professionally in the U.S. Army Dental Reserve Corp. The first step in that direction came in November 1917 when the surgeon general of the United States assigned thirty-four army dental surgeons from all over the country to take a four-week course of advance training at the University of Pennsylvania's Evans Institute given by Dr. Matthew Cryer, "regarded as probably the greatest authority on oral surgery in the world," "Dr. Hermann Prinz, a widely known authority on dental therapeutics, and Dr. James E. Aiguier, a member of the Dental School faculty associated with Dr. Prinz."[70] This four-week course would be repeated with new students from November through March 1918, and Dr. Aiguier became well known to the surgeon general, J. C. Gorgas. In fact, on December 3 he cabled Dr. Aiguier that "he would be investigating the head-gear tomorrow." This will be discussed below.

In December, while continuing to conduct these four-week sessions with

First Lieutenant James Edward Aiguier in the uniform of the United States Army Dental Reserve Corp. in 1918.

Drs. Cryer and Prinz, Dr. Aiguier's status was changed from a civilian to a first lieutenant on active duty in the Dental Reserve Corp of the U.S. Army. With his commission dated December 21, 1917, he became Lt. James Edward Aiguier, but his assignment continued as before throughout the winter of 1918 and ending on April 3 when he went on inactive duty for a time. All the while he still was on the Evans Institute faculty with regular teaching assignments.

The Aiguier Head-Gear was designed by Eddie while working at the Evans Institute prior to November 1917. Its purpose was to hold the jaw in place after severe head injuries so that repair and healing could take place "for supporting bandages and appliances used for face and jaw wounds. For supporting splints, pressure or traction appliances."[71] It was accepted by the Army Dental Corp and used throughout World War I. An example is in the Smithsonian Institute today.

On June 28, 1918, Eddie was called to active duty again by the Dental Reserve Corp, and for the first time he had to stop his teaching at Evans. The term was over anyhow, and he was on the summer holiday period. He was assigned to active duty with Base Hospital No. 115 A. E. F. (Special Head Unit), which at that time was located at Cape May, New Jersey, in the Cape May Hotel. There were thirty-seven officers and two hundred enlisted men in this unit preparing to be shipped to France. The officers, dental and medical, were given duties at Cape May. Eddie was assigned to the group examining the teeth of enlisted men and repairing them if needed. The Hotel was a huge resort building taken over in part by this unit and situated on the ocean beach in a magnificent location. The unit would be there for about a month.

Eddie, with all the others, filled out many forms, one giving the name and address of his nearest of kin in case of injury or death. He named his younger brother, Bertram L. Aiguier of 253 Bainbridge Street, Brooklyn, to be notified in an emergency.

On August 4 he got a two-day leave to say goodbye in Philadelphia to his Evans Institute friends, and on August 15 the Base Hospital No. 115 A. E. F. boarded *Missanabic* in Hoboken, New Jersey, for a two-week voyage to Liverpool, England, arriving on August 29. There followed a train ride to London, to Southampton, a ferry to Cherbourg, France, to Tours and finally to Vichy, a small town in central France, north and west of Lyons. It was well south of Paris and the enemy lines. Vichy was a health resort with a worldwide reputation at that time. Located on the banks of the Allier river, its waters were seen

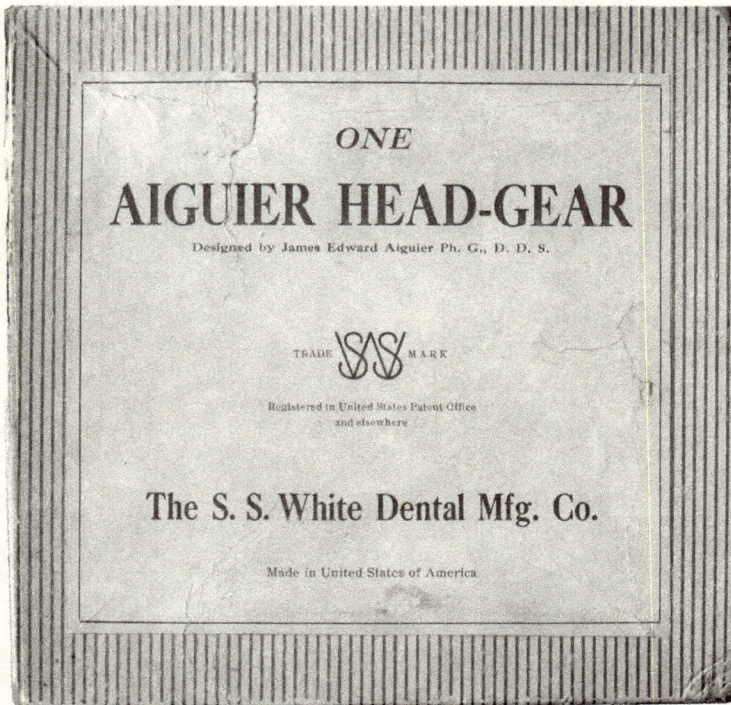

ONE

AIGUIER HEAD-GEAR

Designed by James Edward Aiguier Ph. G., D. D. S.

TRADE SAS MARK

Registered in United States Patent Office
and elsewhere

The S. S. White Dental Mfg. Co.

Made in United States of America

Designed by Lt. Aiguier in 1917, the head-gear was accepted by the Surgeon-General to treat severe head inuries. An example is in the Smithsonian Institute today.

Above, Base Hospital #115 A. E. F. pictured in front of Cape May Hotel, New Jersey, prior to going to France in Summer 1918. James E. Aiguier is in the fourth row, first on the left and marked by him with an arrow. *Below*, the Hotel Ruhl, Vichy, was the location of Base Hospial #115 from September 1918 to January 1919.

to have curative powers. Its springs from deep underground were bicarbonate of soda and were consumed as well as bathed in. Many hotels had grown up around "the Grand Establishment" where the spring water was directed and used. One of these, the Ruhl Hotel (see photograph) was taken over by the French government during the war and became the hospital for four base hospital units, one of which was Base Unit No. 115 A. E. F. It remained there for most of September, all of October, November, and December—four months. The armistice was signed on November 11, so new patients ceased coming soon after that historic day. Fighting had been fierce on the front in September and October when the Allies made their final push across the Ardennes Forest to dislodge the Germans from their trenches. Causalities were heavy at that time and hospitals were filling up with the wounded. At the same time they were filling up with victims of the Spanish flu, which by that fall was killing more people than the war.

Eddie received a seven-day leave upon his request to go to Paris in early January 1919 to visit the hospitals and examine the face work that had been performed on war victims. Dr. Prinz had asked him to find out what he could about trench mouth and its treatment.

On January 14 he received embarkation orders to go to Angers first and then on February 7 to proceed to Camp Porte Foye to board the *SS Rotterdam* for the voyage to Hoboken, New Jersey. Ten days later Eddie was back in the U.S.A. On February 26 he received an honorable discharge at Camp Dix, New Jersey. With it came a Gold Chevron for war service overseas from August 15, 1918 to February 17, 1919—six months.

Highlights of His Career

Should he have been asked to identify his principal life's work, Dr. Aiguier would have said it was being a teacher at the School of Dental Medicine at the University of Pennsylvania. He had been a student there for three years, and except for the year he served in the United States Army Dental Corp, he was on the teaching staff from 1917–1952, a remarkable thirty-five years.

His career included many other facets: an important private practice, founding and operating a dental clinic at the Presbyterian Hospital in Philadelphia, many consultancies, and membership in many dental societies in the U.S. and in Europe. He believed in joining organizations that promoted the field of dental surgery whenever asked. Seldom did he decline an invitation to speak or read a paper that he had written about his profession. He was awarded many medals from groups that he had served both within and outside his field. His family still has this collection of nineteen medals for service, given to him by various institutions. But in the end he was a teacher, and the Evans Institute was his professional home. I will mention only a few highlights, guided by his medals and curriculum vitae. (See Appendix A.)

Dr. Aiguier's first assignment outside Evans came in September 1919 when he was asked to be the visiting dentist at the plant of Joseph Bancroft and Sons in Wilmington, Delaware. He was expected to be available for a half a day, three days a week, to care for the employees of the plant, for which time he accepted $1,500 per annum. He had asked for $2,000 but accepted the smaller amount. Bancroft supplied a small room and a dental chair where he could treat patients. This assignment required him to commute to Wilmington three times a week, which he did on the Pennsylvania Railroad, only a short distance of twenty minutes, allowing him to keep up with his teaching load at Evans.

In 1921, two years later, a new hospital was opened in Philadelphia. It was named the Presbyterian Hospital. Dr. Aiguier and a close friend and oral surgeon from Evans, Dr. Malcolm Carr, were asked to organize the dental department of the new hospital. Dr. Aiguier became the chief of the department. The clinic at Presbyterian opened in June 1922. Both doctors remained there until 1952, but never reduced their lecturing at Evans.

By 1920 Dr. Aiguier had established his own office, treating private patients at 1614 Locust Street, west of Broad Street in downtown Philadelphia. In 1926 he moved to a larger space in the Medical Arts building at Sixteenth Street and Walnut. He remained there for the rest of his practicing life with a secretary and hygienists to look after his patients.

At the Evans Institute, Dr. Aiguier was a professor and lecturer in three areas of dental medicine:

- Materia medica and therapeutics—the medical science concerned with remedies for diseases.
- Oral hygiene
- Stomatology—now called periodontology, the care of gums in

the mouth. With his degree and experience in pharmacology he would lecture on occasion in that as well.

As the dental profession developed in the late nineteenth and early twentieth centuries, dental schools were usually a part of large universities such as Columbia in New York and the University of Pennsylvania in Philadelphia. In addition to these, independent academies were established by learned men in the field to promote and advance the science of a particular aspect of the dental profession. One of these was the Academy of Stomatology in Philadelphia. This was of particular interest to Dr. Hermann Prinz and his protégé Dr. Aiguier, who both became members. Dr. Aiguier was elected president in 1926, and both were active lecturing into the 1940s. Dr. Aiguier was also elected to the American Academy of Periodontology in 1933. This was a national organization devoted to diseases of the mouth. He became president of this one in 1952, making him the leader of the field in the country.

Dr. Aiguier was a consultant in dental surgery to the Pennsylvania Hospital, Mental and Nervous Diseases, Philadelphia, from 1917–1958; and to the Abington Memorial Hospital, 1924–1958, in Abington, Pennsylvania, a suburb of Philadelphia.

Dr. Aiguier also became a member of many dental organizations. Unlike the consultancies for which he would get a fee, the societies expected his teaching expertise in the form of a lecture or a paper. He gladly gave his time to their programs and activities. Several required his travel to places away from Philadelphia. Some of these were:

- Fellow, American College of Dentistry, F. A. C. D.
- Nonresident fellow, New York Academy of Dentistry
- Chairman of publicity, International Dental Congress held in Philadelphia in 1926
- Chairman, American Dental Association, section on periodontology
- Member, Penn State Dental Society
- Member, International College of Dentistry
- Member and Grand Master, Delta Sigma Delta, the national dental fraternity

1. American Legion
2. Society of Colonial Wars
3. Sons of Revolution
4. Military Order Foreign Wars
5. World War I–service pin
6. Medal–service France (star–active duty–WWI)
7. Medal World War II–Selective Service System
8. Phi Chi Columbia
9. Delta Sigma Delta "U of P"
10. American College of Dentists
11. Omicron Kappa Upsilon
12. Cryer Honor Society
13. Sigma Xi "U of P"
14. ETA Sigma Sigma (honor)
15. Caduceus–Dental Corps
16. Delta Sigma Delta Pledge Pin
17. Masonic Pin
18. Bar–sevice WWII
19. Caduceus–D

The collection of nineteen pins and medals received by Dr. Aiguier during his lifetime, mounted on a plaque.

Other honors he received in his profession:

- Sigma Xi – Honorary Scientific society
- Matthew H. Cryer Society of Oral Surgery – undergraduate
- Edwin T. Darby Dental Society – undergraduate honorary
- Omicron Kappa Upsilon – national dental honorary society established in 1915 by Northwestern University
- Eta Sigma Sigma – national honorary in oral surgery

Other Interests

Outside the field of dentistry, Dr. Aiguier belonged to several organizations both national and local. In 1909, while still living in New York City, he joined the Evangelist Lodge #600 of the F. & A. Masons, New York State branch, and became a life member in 1940. A certificate was sent to him at his retirement home in College Manor, Maryland, honoring his sixty years of service as a Freemason.

For service to his country:

- The Military Order of Foreign Wars 1927
- World War I: service award
- France, service medal; active duty World War I
- Selective Service Medal—World War II—for service on the Medical Advisory Board 1941–1947
- American Legion, the post at Merion, Pennsylvania, which he joined in 1934

Genealogy:

- The Pennsylvania Society of Sons of the Revolution
- The Society of Colonial Wars of the State of New York

He was also a member of the Union League Club in Philadelphia and the University Club in Philadelphia and New York City.

Dr. Aiguier with his family on the occasion of his daughter Eugénie's debutante party at the Barclay Hotel in Philadelphia on June 17, 1947. Standing, *left to right*:John Atlee Light Thomas (Jack), Antoinette Aiguier (Ann), James Edward Aiguier (Favie), Eugénie Aiguier (Genie), and Frank Howard Thomas (Howard). Seated on left, Virginia Light Aiguier (Mater) and right, Madeline Thomas (Babs, wife of Howard).

Personal and Family

The following article appeared in the Delta Sigma Delta-Desmos (the fraternity news magazine) of November 1923:

> Wonders, upon wonders—will they ever cease! In my August letter I accused our Grand Master [Dr. Aiguier] of being a confirmed bachelor. I always thought he knew better than to lead a single life, and now my thought is confirmed, for Cupid's dart has hit him. I have been unable to learn the lady's name, but we all want her to know that she has found a "Prince" for a husband. They are now at home at the Powelton Apartments, 35th Street and Powelton Avenue, Philadelphia, Pa. "Ed" assures me that the latch string is always out. May their married life be long and happy.[72]

On September 26, 1923, James Edward Aiguier married Mary Virginia Light. They had two daughters: Antoinette, born January 22, 1925; and Eugénie, born October 25, 1929. Mrs. Aiguier had previously been married to Frank Howard Thomas and had two sons—Frank Howard Thomas Jr. and John Atlee Light Thomas—before her husband's death. With the birth of Ann Aiguier the family moved to 21 Lodges Lane in Cynwyd, a suburb of Philadelphia, outside City line, and after Genie was born they moved to 10 Radcliff Road nearby, where they remained until after both daughters had married and moved away.

His Death

James Edward Aiguier—Eddie to his parents, teachers, and colleagues; Jim to his wife; and Favie to his children and grandchildren—died on November 3, 1977, at the age of ninety-four. He died at College Manor in Lutherville, Maryland, the retirement home where he had been living for four or five years.

In a letter to his daughter Eugénie A. Havemeyer he said, "It is my desire that my remains be buried in the nearest United States Military Cemetery." She was able to find a grave site at the Long Island National Cemetery in Farmingdale, New York, where military-style monuments are the same for every soldier and officer. The inscription on his reads:

James Edward Aiguier
1st Lieutenant
U. S. Army
World War I
October 18, 1883–November 3, 1977
Base Hospital
115 A. E. F.

In Memoriam

From the time he entered the Evans Institute of the University of Pennsylvania in the fall of 1914 to his death in 1977—sixty-three years—Dr. James Edward Aiguier, Ph.G, D.D.S, F.A.C.D, devoted himself to the field of dentistry, becoming one of its leading dental surgeons during much of the twentieth century. Especially in the field of periodontology, which was new at the time, he became recognized by all his colleagues as being at the top of the profession.

In the volume Colonial and Revolutionary Lineages of America there is a chapter about Dr. Aiguier, including a photographic portrait of him at the age of sixty, his curriculum vitae, and a substantial amount about his genealogy, particularly the Demarest, Powles, Christopher, Wood, and Webb families, ancestors of his mother. At the time the volume was published in 1943 much less was known about his paternal forbearers before the marriage of Jean Baptiste Aiguier to Mary Cecile Arnoux in 1816. Hopefully this story has filled in that gap.

Favie on board *Mouette* cruising on the Great South Bay, summer 1961.

APPENDIX A

Curriculum Vitae (as prepared by Dr. Aiguier in 1958)

Aiguier, James E., Ph. G., D. D. S., F. A. C. D.

University of Pennsylvania, D. D. S., 1917.

Columbia University, Ph. G., 1905.

Assistant Professor, Oral Hygiene.   ) Dental School,University of

Director Courses in Oral Hygiene.   ) Pennsylvania.
)- Member Teaching Staff
Lecturer Materia Medica and Therapeutics.)   1917 to 1952.

Dental Surgeon and Chief of Dental Department,
Presbyterian Hospital, Philadelphia, 1921–52.

Dental Surgeon, Pennsylvania Hospital, Mental and Nervous Diseases,
Philadelphia. 1917–58.

Active Consultant, Abington Memorial Hospital, Abington, Pennsylvania. 1924–
1958.

The American Board of Periodontology. 1942.

Honorary Member:
American Dental Society of Europe. 1948.
Southern Academy of Periodontology.
North Carolina Dental Association. 1941.
Yokosuke and Miura Dental Association– Japan 1956.

Fellow:
American Academy of Periodontology. 1962.
American College of Dentists. 1937. F.A.C.D.
Non-resident, New York Academy of Dentistry. 1929.
International College of Dentists. 1929.

Past President:
Dental Alumni Society, University of Pennsylvania. 1923.
Academy of Stomatology, Philadelphia. 1925–1926.
Pan American Odontological Association. 1950.
American Academy of Periodontology. 1952.
Eta Sigma Sigma, Mathew H. Cryer Chapter (Honorary).

Darby Dental Society (Undergraduate). 1917.
Past Grand Master, Philadelphia Auxiliary Delta Sigma Delta. 1920.

Chairman Publicity Committee, 7th International Dental Congress. 1926.

Chairman Section on Periodontology, American Dental Association. 1949.

Chairman Section on Local Anesthesia, Dental Clinic Club of Philadelphia. 1925–1952.

Member Committee on Dental Preparations, National Formulary 6th Edition. 1926. And 7th Edition. 1936.

Executive Committee, Pennsylvania Emergency Child Health Committee of Pennsylvania State Medical Society. 1933–1942.

Commission to First Lieutenant in Dental Reserve Corp., U.S. Army. 1917, Foreign Duty.

Delta Sigma Delta (Life Member)–National Dental Fraternity.

Sigma Xi. March 1917–Honorary in Science.

Omicron Kappa Upsilon–National Dental (Honorary).

Life member Evangelist Lodge #600
F&A Masons of New York State. 1909.

Union League Club of Philadelphia. 1933.

University Club of Philadelphia. 1922.

University Club of New York City.

Military Order of Foreign Wars. 1927.

Selective Service Medal, as member of Medical Advisory Board in World War II, signed by Harry S. Truman. 1941–1947.

Dates and Gravesites*

Children of Joseph and Marie Chartier and their Spouses:

Pierre Chartier, b. Sep 1756, d. 25 Dec 1829.

Polly Robinett Chartier, spouse, b. 1763, date of death unknown.

Jean Chartier, b. Apr 1758, d. 25 Jun 1832.

Sally Robinett Chartier, spouse, birth and death dates unknown.

Cecile Chartier Arnoux, b. 1 Aug 1770, d. 1 Jan 1840.

Jean François Arnoux, spouse, b. 1752, d. 1805.

Family of Jean Baptisite Aiguier buried at Green-Wood Cemetery, Brooklyn, New York, section 75, plot 3976, on top of the catacombs:

Aiguier, Mary Cecile Arnoux, b. circa 1791, d. 30 May 1850.

Aiguier, Jean Baptiste, b. 1769, d. 29 Sep 1851.

Aiguier, Mary Eliza Decker, first wife of Gabriel Aiguier, b. 1831, d. Oct 1855.

Aiguier, Joanna Cochran, second wife of Gabriel Aiguier, b. 1861, d. Oct 1886.

Aiguier, John B., Jr., son of Jean Baptiste Aiguier, b. 11 Oct 1821, d. 17 May 1890.

Aiguier, Gabriel, son of Jean Baptiste Aiguier, b. 3 Oct 1828, d. 6 Dec 1903.

Aiguier, Eleanor Cochran, daughter of Gabriel Aiguier, b. 1861, d. Apr 1924.

Sweeney, Vaiden B., son-in-law of Gabriel Aiguier, b. 23 Jul 1857, d. 3 Aug 1937.

Sweeney, Lizzie Aiguier, daughter of Gabriel Aiguier, b. 1 Dec 1859, d. 16 Sep 1939.

Aiguier, Bertram L., great grandson of Jean Baptiste Aiguier, b. 22 Dec 1885, d. Jul 1950.

Aiguier, Martha W., wife of Bertram Aiguier and daughter of Vaiden Sweeney, b. Oct 1887, d. Feb 1971.

---

*   The listing of Aiguiers and Arnouxs buried at Green-Wood Cemetery and Demarests at the Moravian Cemetery is not a complete one.

Family of Arnoux buried at Green-Wood Cemetery, Brooklyn, New York,

Section 35, plot 4250:

Arnoux, Anthony, son of Jean François Arnoux, b. 9 Oct 1788, d. 20 May 1872.

Arnoux, Gertrude Freeland, his wife, b. 4 Feb 1796, d. 24 Feb 1875.

Section 7, plot 9044*:

Arnoux, Gabriel A., brother of Anthony, b. 19 Jan 1805, d. 20 Jan 1855.

Arnoux, Ann Kennett., his wife, b. Aug 1808, d. Feb 1855.

Family buried at the Moravian Cemetery on Staten Island, New York:

Aiguier, James Kurley, son of Gabriel, husband of Lauretta Demarest Aiguier, b. 13 May 1850, d. 21 Dec 1892.

Aiguier, Lauretta Demarest, wife of James K. Aiguier, daughter of Abraham J. and Sarah C. Demarest, b. 9 Dec 1858, d. 1 Jan 1915.

Demarest, Sarah Christopher, wife of Abraham Demarest, mother of Lauretta, b. 12 Dec 1837, d. 12 Aug 1915.

Demarest, Abraham J., husband of Sarah Christopher, father of Lauretta, b. 27 Apr 1833, d. 18 Jan 1916.

Aiguier, Percy Gabriel, son of James K. and Lauretta Aiguier, brother of James Edward Aiguier, b. 18 Aug 1881, d. 25 Feb 1925.

James Edward Aiguier, b. 18 Oct 1883, d. 3 Nov 1977, is buried in section G, number 6692-C at the Long Island National Cemetery in Farmingdale, New York.

---

*   No gravestones are remaining.

A Partial Family Tree of the ancestors of James E. Aiguier

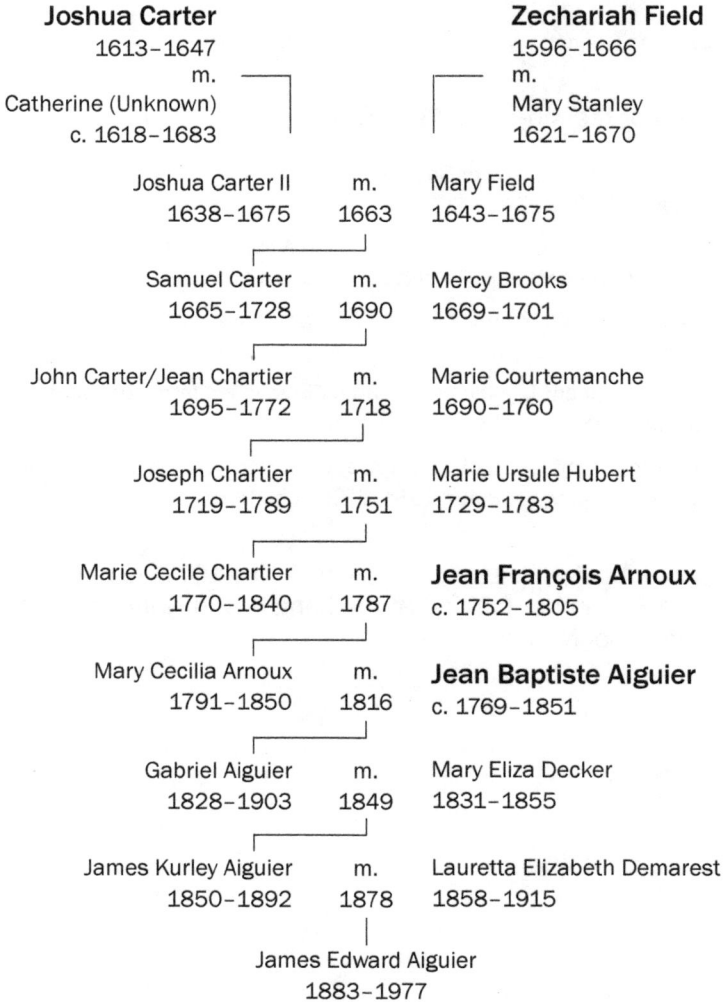

Joshua Carter		**Zechariah Field**
1613–1647		1596–1666
m.		m.
Catherine (Unknown)		Mary Stanley
c. 1618–1683		1621–1670

Joshua Carter II	m.	Mary Field
1638–1675	1663	1643–1675

Samuel Carter	m.	Mercy Brooks
1665–1728	1690	1669–1701

John Carter/Jean Chartier	m.	Marie Courtemanche
1695–1772	1718	1690–1760

Joseph Chartier	m.	Marie Ursule Hubert
1719–1789	1751	1729–1783

Marie Cecile Chartier	m.	**Jean François Arnoux**
1770–1840	1787	c. 1752–1805

Mary Cecilia Arnoux	m.	**Jean Baptiste Aiguier**
1791–1850	1816	c. 1769–1851

Gabriel Aiguier	m.	Mary Eliza Decker
1828–1903	1849	1831–1855

James Kurley Aiguier	m.	Lauretta Elizabeth Demarest
1850–1892	1878	1858–1915

James Edward Aiguier
1883–1977

Published in *The New York Genealogical and Biographical Record*.
Volume 133, January 2002.

CONWAY ARMSTRONG CONFESSES

The following advertisement was published in the *Commercial Advertiser*, New York, Saturday, 3 June 1815, p. 3 (and other dates). Henry B. Hoff found this while reading the newspaper on microfilm at the American Antiquarian Society, Worcester, Massachusetts.

NEW-YORK, May 29th, 1815.

☞ I, CONWAY ARMSTRONG, being deeply sensible of the great injury done to MARY ARNOUX, in having married her at a time when my lawful wife, BARBARY ARMSTRONG, was living, of which she, Mary Arnoux, was entirely ignorant, do, in the presence of the Rev. Mr. LYELL, Record of Christ Church in this city, (who solemnized the rites of matrimony between us on the 21st of April 1810) and the undersigned witnesses, with sorrow confess my crime, most earnestly entreat her forgiveness, and promise henceforward on *all occasions*, and to *all persons* who may be interested, to acknowledge *her innocence* and *my most flagrant imposture* in this affair.

THOMAS LYELL,
   Rector of Christ Church, N.Y.

GERTRUDE ARNOUX,

AUGUSTE LEMOYNE,   } Witnesses.

DAVID BOARD,

ANTHONY ARNOUX,

N.B. Editors of newspapers friendly to the cause of virtue, are respectfully invited to give the above advertisement *one insertion*.

SOURCE NOTES

1. David Hackett Fischer, *Albion's Seed: Four British Folkways in America* (New York, Oxford: Oxford University Press, 1989), 31.
2. Fischer, 16, 205.
3. Ibid., 16.
4. Thistlethwaite, Frank, *The Dorset Pilgrims* (London: Barrie & Jenkins, 1989), 60.
5. Bailyn, Bernard, *The Barbarous Years* (New York: Alfred A. Knopf, 2012), 389.
6. Cave, Alfred A., *The Pequot War* (Amherst, Massachusetts, 1996).
7. Field Genealogy, 99.
8. Ibid.
9. Ibid.
10. Nathaniel Philbrick, *Mayflower: A Story of Courage, Community, and War* (New York: Viking, 2006), xv.
11. Evan Haefeli and Kevin Sweeney, *Captors and Captives: The 1704 French and Indian Raid on Deerfield* (Amherst: University of Massachusetts Press, 2003), 115.
12. Ibid., 240.
13. Ibid.
14. Ibid., 248, 249.
15. Wikipedia, "Hazen's Regiment."
16. "American National Biography" for Moses Hazen.
17. Kenneth O. Morgan, ed., *The Oxford History of Britain* (New York, Oxford: Oxford University Press, 1988), 240.
18. Tom Pocock, *Battle for Empire: The Very First World War 1756–63* (London: Michael O'Mara Books Ltd., 1998), 13.
19. Richard M. Ketchum, *Victory at Yorktown: The Campaign that Won the Revolution* (New York: Henry Holt and Company, 2004), 15.
20. Ibid., 16.
21. Ibid., 172.
22. Ketchum, 10.
23. Ibid., 30.
24. Ibid., 31.
25. Ketchum, 26.
26. Ketchum, 43.
27. Ibid., 44.
28. Ketchum, 81.
29. Ibid.
30. Ibid., 84.

31. Ibid., 135.
32. Ibid., 140–141.
33. *New York Times* Op-Ed, 7/14/11.
34. Ketchum, 178.
35. Ketchum, 131, 132.
36. Ketchum, 143.
37. Ibid, 183.
38. Ketchum, 209.
39. Ibid.
40. Ibid, 212.
41. Ketchum, 217.
42. Ibid., 224.
43. Wikipedia, "Hazen's Regiment."
44. Ketchum, 236.
45. Ibid.
46. Ibid., 239.
47. Ibid., 240.
48. Ibid., 242.
49. Ibid., 244.
50. Ibid., 247.
51. *North American Review*, Volume 206, *No. 740* (July 1917), 161–176.
52. *Times of London*, March 2012.
53. Ketchum, 275.
54. Ibid., 283.
55. James Thomas Flexner, *Washington: The Indispensable Man* (Boston: Little, Brown and Company, 1974), 179.
56. "Drumbeat" Spring 2011, Volume 29, No. 1.
57. Ketchum, 285.
58. The quotes in this section are from sworn statements by various parties in 1818, 1819, 1837, and 1839, recorded many years after the events described took place. They are found in the records of the State of Vermont, Addison County.
59. Benjamin W. Dwight, *The History of the Descendants of Elder John Strong of Northampton, Massachusetts* (Albany, New York: John Munsel, 1871, vol. 11), 1015.
60. Records of Addison County, Vermont.
61. Early History of St. Peter's Church, Vergennes, Vermont, 5.
62. Op. cit. Addison County Records.
63. Op. cit. Dwight, 1016.
64. *Les Français au Quebec 1765–1865* states: "Arnoux, Jean François, originally of the parish of La Major [Lost in Canada says Saint-Marie-Majeure], city of Marseille, was born of the union of Jean François Arnoux, a surgeon major, and Anne Monestier. He arrived in Canada around 1785..." "He wed at L'Acadie, 20 May 1787, Cecile Chartier, daughter of Joseph Chartier and Ursule Hubert. Between 1791 and 1794, three chil-

dren were born of that union of which Cecile was baptized at L'Acadie on 8 June 1791. After 1794 there was no sign of this family."

65. Application of William Perry Baldwin for membership in the Sons of the American Revolution.

66. Because he had been born in Canada and lived for a time outside the United States in 1810–1812, Anthony Arnoux had to register in order to own property in New York, which he did on July 28, 1818. "Early New York Naturalizations – 1792 – 1840," Arnoux, Anthony, 1818, merchant tailor, subject of Great Britain.

67. Edwin G. Burrows and Mike Wallace, *Gotham: A History of New York City* (New York: Oxford University Press, 1999), 606.

68. Ibid.

69. Ibid., 889.

70. *The Public Ledger*, Philadelphia, Sunday, November 11, 1917.

71. The Head-Gear Manual.

72. Delta Sigma Delta Desmos, November 1923.

ILLUSTRATIONS

Illustrations not listed above are in the family collection.

BIBLIOGRAPHY

Books

Bailyn, Bernard. *The Barbarous Years*. New York: Alfred A. Knoft, 2012.

Burrows, Edwin G., and Mike Wallace. *Gotham: A History of New York City*. Oxford University Press, 1999.

Cave, Alfred A., *The Pequot War*. Amherst: University of Massachusetts Press, 1996.

Dwight, Benjamin W. *The History of the Descendants of Elder John Strong of Northampton, Massachusetts*. Albany, New York: John Mansel, 1871.

Fischer, David Hackett. *Albion's Seed*. New York, Oxford: Oxford University Press, 1989.

Flexner, James Thomas. *Washington, The Indispensable Man*. Boston: Little, Brown and Company, 1974.

Haefli, Evan, and Kevin Sweeney. *Captors and Captives*. Amherst and Boston: University of Massachusetts Press, 2005.

Havemeyer, Harry W. *The Story of Jonas Mapes*. New York: privately printed, 2008.

Jackson, Kenneth T., ed. *New York City*. New Haven, Yale University Press, 1995.

Ketchum, Richard M., *Victory at Yorktown*. New York: Henry Holt and Company, 2004.

Morgan, Kenneth O., ed. *Oxford History of Britain*. Oxford University Press, 1988.

Philbrick, Nathaniel. *Mayflower*. New York: Viking, 2006.

Pocock, Tom. *Battle for Empire: The Very First World War, 1756–1763*. London: Michael O'Mara Books Ltd., 1998.

Shea, John Gilmary, ed. *The Operations of the French Fleet Under Count De Grasse in 1781–2*. New York, Bradford Club Series, 1864.

Taylor, Alan. *American Colonies, the Settlement of North America to 1800*. New York, Viking, 2001.

Thistlethwaite, Frank. *Dorset Pilgrims*. London, Barrie & Jenkins, 1989.

Encyclopedias and Genealogies

American National Biography.

Colonial and Revolutionary Lineages of America. The American Historical Company, New York, 1943.

Demarest, Mary A. and William H. S. *The Demarest Family*. New Brunswick, New Jersey, 1938.

France, *Les Combattants Français de la Guerre Americaine, 1778–1783*. Paris, 1903. Translated in Washington D.C., 1905.

Fournier, Marcel. *Les Français au Quebec, 1765–1865*. Québec, Septentrion, 1995.

Pierce, Frederick Clifton. *Field Genealogy, Volume 1*. Chicago: Hammond Press, 1901.

Stiles, Henry R. *The History and Genealogies of Ancient Windsor, Vol I*. Hartford: Press of the Case, Lockwood & Brainard Company, 1891.

Stokes, I. N. Phelps. *The Iconography of Manhattan Island, 1498-1909*, Volume 3. New York : Robert H. Dodd, 1918.

The Great Migration Begins: Immigrants to New England 1620–1633, Volume I. Boston: NEHGS, 1995.

Records, Articles, and Newspapers

Application for Membership—Sons of the American Revolution for William Perry Baldwin, Jr.

"Drumbeat," *Sons of the Revolution, Volume 29*, 2011.

Early History of St. Peter's Church in Vergennes.

Early New York Naturalizations 1792–1840.

Family Records of Green-Wood Cemetery.

National Census Records.

New York City Directories.

New York Evening Post.

New York Genealogical and Biographical Society Record. Volume 141, April 2010.

New York Herald.

New York Times.

North American Review. Volume 206, No. 740.

Records of Addison County, State of Vermont.

INDEX

Italic page numbers refer to illustrations.

www.ingramcontent.com/pod-product-compliance
Lightning Source LLC
Chambersburg PA
CBHW021825090426
42811CB00032B/2018/J